1997

AFRICAN DEVELOPMENT DILEMMA

The Big Debate

Samuel M. Muriithi

University Press of America, Inc.
Lanham • New York • London

Copyright © 1997 by
University Press of America,® Inc.
4720 Boston Way
Lanham, Maryland 20706

3 Henrietta Street
London, WC2E 8LU England

Library of Congress Cataloging-in-Publication Data

Muriithi, Samuel M.
African development dilemma : the big debate / by Samuel M.
Muriithi.
p.   cm.
Includes bibliographical references.
1. Africa--economic conditions. 2. Africa--Dependency on foreign
countries. 3. Africa--Social conditions. I. Title.
HC800.M843 1996   338.96--dc20   96-41720 CIP

ISBN 0-7618-0546-X (cloth: alk. ppr.)
ISBN 0-7618-0547-8 (pbk. : alk. ppr.)

*DEDICATED TO ALL PATRIOTIC
AFRICANS*

TABLE OF CONTENTS

PREFACE

Who is an African? Is he a normal human being or a less human being? Can he develop his continent to an acceptable level? And is an African really responsible for all the messes present in Africa today? Are there other persons or forces which have made things worse in Africa? These and many other questions face the world today as Africa continues to deteriorate in all sectors; political, social, and economic. Civil wars, hunger, corruption, poverty increase and low investments have become the order of the day. Africa is in a state of despair and something needs to be done.

This book seeks to discuss the above issues as they relate to development of Africa. The arguments presented are based on the human, social, economic, natural and political perspectives.

Presenting my arguments in form of a debate, I have analysed the controversial issues in Africa today, and have provided recommendations as to what Africa needs. Some specific matters addressed in the book include the following:

a) Are Africans capable of developing Africa? This question stems from the concern raised by many scholars and politicians that an African is a lesser human being compared to other races. I have examined the issue deeply to show why an African is termed as so. This is an issue that has undermined Africans' dignity and self-worth, thus contributing to the negative attitudes from other races.

b) How has natural calamities affected development in Africa? This question is key because most African governments have blamed nature as responsible for under-development of the continent. In this book, *African Development Dilemma: The Big Debate*, I have explored the cause of nature-related problems and the African governments' role. It is by effective planning and seriousness of the implementors that the crisis would be solved.

c) Did slavery contribute to under-development of Africa? Considering that millions of Africans were taken as slaves, many people argue that this was a major drawback to African development. Those taken as slaves were capable men and women who would have played significant role in the development of the continent. Whether things would be different if slavery did not take place is a major argument addressed.

d) How has the West continued to hinder African development? There is a strong view among African leaders and economists that both Europe and the United States have continued to exploit Africa. Through political manipulation and economical ideologies, both powers have influenced African development. By using foreign democracy, financial aid, dictatorship, increasing multinational activities and cultural changes, the West determines development trend in Africa. The book brings the controversy as to whether the West is needed in Africa or not.

Anyone interested in the political, economic and political development in Africa will find this book an eye opener and a reliable source. It is a book that politicians, leaders, managers, economists, development agents, college students and professors of political science and economics would desire to read.

The goal of writing this book will be achieved if the readers gain new insights into Africa's dilemma and hopefully take appropriate action to develop the continent.

Sam Muriithi, 1996

ACKNOWLEDGEMENTS

One of the great pleasures of writing is the opportunity to learn from many sources. The sources include experts, practitioners, politicians, and colleagues. Although the preparation of this book has demanded much time, energy and contributions from numerous areas, it is a great joy to have it finally in the hands of the target audience. To all those who assisted in one way or another, I say thank you. It is impossible to mention all the contributors, but their effort is worth noted. However, I owe a debt of gratitude to the following friends, colleagues, institutions and authorities.

Inspirers: I'm greatly inspired by patriotic African leaders who have fought for an African independence and recognition, both locally and internationally. Specifically, I owe much thanks to key leaders in this noble task among them being: President Daniel Arap Moi, Kenya; President Nelson Mandela, Republic of South Africa, President Yoweri Museveni, Uganda, Mwalimu Julius Nyerere, Former president of Tanzania, Bishop Desmon Tutu, South Africa, the late Mzee Jomo Kenyatta, Kenya, and Kwame Nkurumah, Ghana. Other inspirers are African scholars, journalists and politicians, all who have defended an African and criticized accordingly. You have all been good models of true Africans.

Professors: Ernest Najoli, Commerce Department, Daystar University. Bokoo Omwansa, Community Development, Daystar University. Levi Obonyo, Communication Department, Daystar University. Thank you for taking the time and effort to read through the manuscript and offering constructive insights.

Editors: Pauline Muriithi, my dear wife. Dorothy Wanjiku, Catherine Ndungu, all of Daystar University. Typists: Sarah Malaki, Grace Ngigi and Beatrice Omonding. Thanks for your time and skills without which the book would be incomplete. It is through your devotion and commitment that the book took shape.

Students: Many thanks to my students especially those who took the course, "African Economic Problems", at Daystar University. Most of the ideas in the book have been tested and discussed in this course. The book should acts as a guide to the students as they leave school and take charge in developing Africa.

Institutions: Finally, I'm grateful to all those institutions that allowed me to use their facilities. Among them are Daystar University Library, Nairobi

University Library, Nation Newspaper, The Computer Drome and various persons and institutions that granted permissions to reprint certain sections.

You have all made significant contributions toward this book completion. Thanks again.

CHAPTER ONE

AN AFRICAN IS A LESSER HUMAN BEING

The African has been taught to abandon his old ways,   yet he is not accepted in the world even when he has   mastered its ways. There seems to be no bridge, and   this is the source of his terrible loneliness (CMT,   New York 1962).

INTRODUCTION

During my undergraduate, one of my great friends was from a central African country. We did many things together; we studied   together, shared domestic matters and even took several Christian   missions together. I respected him especially for his age. He was a father of four and I was single, so I received some counseling on how to nurse my wife and family when I get married. Of course like any other man, I enjoyed such talks. We had a father-son like relationship. Not that I was the only one benefiting, he also enjoyed my company because I taught him how to   deal with some difficult courses, especially Mathematics and English. I was not very good at these subjects (my former teachers would tell you so), but I served his needs and he was glad.   To date, the relationship still exists although my friend is many miles away and busy with his country's development.

From the above explanation, it may seem that the relation ship was good from the start. However, we were first enemies. Not that my friend knew I was his enemy. He was always a friend from the beginning. But I saw him as an enemy and inhuman. In fact I feared him and avoided his company. It is easy to say I was his enemy although I never made it known to him or others. It took a long time for me to change my attitude towards him. I hated him for who he was. At first I thought he was a fellow human being like the rest of us. However, this changed when one day he shared with me about how they deal with monkeys in his country.

"We love monkeys," my friend once said as we talked about our different diets. I told him that my community loved maize and we also enjoyed beef and chicken. My friend was astonished, as his eyes widened and his mouth opened. I was surprised at his reaction and I wondered whether it was me or our diet that had surprised him. Was it me or our dear diet? But he was quick to respond. "You mean you have no monkeys in Kenya?" he asked quite amazed. "We have monkeys in the forests and in the national parks," I answered. "Do you want me to take you there to see some?" I asked. "No! No!" My friend noted quickly. "We have many monkeys at home. I just wondered why you don't like monkeys," he responded a bit defensive. "No I don't mean that," he explained. "I mean, do you .... you mean you don't eat monkey meat?" "What? Monkey meat? Who would eat it? This is an abomination to the society. How can anyone eat monkey meat?" Instead of being shocked by my reaction he smiled and said, "Monkey meat is nice and delicious, there is no other meat that is that good". I could not believe what he said. You mean there are people on earth who eat monkeys?. But a monkey looks like a human being. Eating a monkey is like eating a "person", I thought. My friend told me even how they invade a forest to catch monkeys. He said "during monkey hunting, a group of villagers would surround a bush where the monkey is hiding. The monkey would be scared and would climb a tree. Some villagers would climb the same tree while others surrounded the tree with a net to trap the monkey if it tried to escape. When it jumped from the tree, the villagers would catch it and club it to death." You should have seen my friend demonstrate how the monkey is caught. "It is then butchered and shared among the villagers," he concluded. A monkey is what a chicken is in my community, he observed.

From that time, I thought my friend was a cannibal. To me a monkey is like a person, after all, science says both humans and monkeys belong to the same species. It is also thought that the monkey species are in the process of evolving to be human. For some reasons my friend did not appeal to me any more until later in our school years. My attitude changed when I read a book entitled *Peace Child* by Don Richard. In this book, the key communities hunted each other for meat. In fact, by befriending a person of another community, the friend was said to be fattened for a meal. Here I saw a community worse than my friend's. If my friend came from such a community, I would have been eaten a long time ago. Later in a course entitled the "Integrated Studies", I learnt the need to respect other communities as I respected mine. I had a problem accepting this but I came to realize that what I   may dislike in my community could be what another community would died to eat. I have learnt to respect others as fellow human beings irrespective of their tribe, diet, race or origin. What they eat, where they live or how they worship may vary but we are all equal. They may live in the bush or in a good home, but that does not make them less or more human. Among major religions on earth, for example, Christianity, all human beings are God's creation and are equal. No particular culture or race is superior to another. All are equal in God's sight.

THE INFERIORITY OF AN AFRICAN

The equality of human beings irrespective of their origin or race is an easily stated principle but one that is difficult to practice. At least it seems like this. There exists a big difference between world races: Whites, Asians, Africans, Jews, American-Indians and the Aborigines of Australia. These groups treat each other differently. While some consider themselves to be superior, others are termed as inferior and less human. Terms like primitive, savages, cannibals and slaves have been used to refer to lower classified races. Terms like gods, masters, lords and superiors have been used to refer to those classified and placed at the top of the hierarchy of race groupings. The groupings have existed over centuries.

The focus of this chapter is to explore how an African has been treated and termed as a lesser human being by the White community. Many examples exist to make this fact clear. An African has fallen a victim of discrimination and condemnation, just because of his color. Being Black is being "inferior," "evil," and "dirty".   It is being useless".

" It is being an "animal". Being Black means that an African is biologically, intellectually and socially inferior. It means an African cannot make any intellectual decisions and so the Whites have taken the burden of making the "right" decisions for him. The decisions as to what is good for him has been controversial for generations among the Westerners. Can the Africans really be democratic without our assistance and intellectual intervention? How can we make an African "civilized"? How can we make sure his damn religion is replaced with God given religion. Can the African be economically independent? Would Africa be safe if it was left alone?

All these and many other questions could be asked and have been asked. These stem from the fact that an African is considered incapable of developing Africa. The move has been to remove Africa from an African and replace it with a "Western person", a civilized person.

From time immemorial, the African person has been considered to be less human in comparison to other races. Let us explore some of the practices that demonstrate the point on how an African is perceived by the West.

THE MISSIONARY-EXPLORERS' BIAS

Missionaries and explorers are the key persons who made Africa's inferiority known to the world. The goal of the missionaries was to spread the Good News, the Gospel of Jesus Christ, to the Africans. One of the known missionaries was Dr. David Livingstone, the British medical missionary who spent many years in Africa. Dr. Livingstone has been recognized for opening way for other missionaries. He has also been associated with opening Africa for European commercial activities. While little has been mentioned about Dr. Livingstone's ill-treatment of Africans, the opposite was true for his friend Henry Morton Stanley who was sent to find Livingstone in 1871. Although an orphan and abandoned when young, Stanley became very successful under his foster father's care. He eventually became a journalist, a career that made James Gordon Bennett, publisher of the *New York Herald,* send him to Africa in 1871. This particular trip made Stanley not only famous in America and Europe, but also a legend. It is after this journey that he made a trans-African journey that took him 999 days. The journey led to the authorship of his book entitled *Through the Dark Continent,* a term still used today to refer to Africa. Like the book's title, Stanley saw nothing "good" in Africa. His biases against Africa were expressed in many of his meetings and writings. At one point he hated his being an explorer in Africa for he "detest the land most heartily" (Unger, 1989:42). Everything said or written by him about Africa reflected hate and pride. Referring to an encounter with a group of Africans he noted:

> A skirmish in their streets, drive them pell-mell into the woods beyond, and level their ivory temples; with frantic haste I fire the huts, and end the scene by towing the canoes into mid-stream setting them a drift (Unger, 1989: 42)

Referring to Africans as unfriendly, he observed that "... ". . . . natives are so wild here .... they will not stay to be questioned, they are to be captured .... and made friends by force" (p. 42). I wonder how friends can be made by force, but that was Stanley's method.

In Europe and America, Stanley saw himself as the African's friend and promoter. He saw Africa as designed by God for Western use. He advocated that God had intended that Africa "should be reserved until the fullness of time for something higher than a nursery for birds and store-place for reptiles" (p.42) With this view, Stanley was not impressed when he failed to convince the British Government and businessmen to be more involved in the affairs of the Africans. Refusing to give up, Stanley turned to Belgium. His intention was to see the scramble for Africa convened at Berlin in German. He was successful in providing a personal service to King Leopold. The King regarded the Congo basin as his private property. On the King's behalf, Stanley signed treaties and established outposts in the bush. It was from the French explorer Count Savorgan de Brazza that Stanley received great competition over Africa exploration. In 1884 however, he became an advisor to the American delegation during Berlin Conference convened to settle disputes over the Congo. This gave him a significant role in the scramble, a role which definitely made him promote African inferiority abroad.

Other missionaries like Livingstone are praised for the spread of the Gospel all over Africa, especially South of the Sahara. Many played a key role in raising the inhabitants' standard of living. Thanks to those who provided medical facilities to reduce the mortality rate especially among children. Some are also remembered for their sincere motives of spreading the Gospel of Christ. However, some missionaries' behavior was contrary to Christ's humility and love for all people. They preached one message but practiced another.

One of the things they promoted was the Western civilization to serve as the model for living for all communities. The African form of worship was condemned as evil and suspicious. Drums were removed from churches as a form of cleaning the African society from evil spirits. Those who resisted the removal were either ex-communicated from the churches. Otherwise forced to divorce all other wives and leave only one as advocated by "Christianity." The children fathered by such husbands were considered to be products of sin. This became a source of conflict between the two cultures, the African and the Western cultures. This led to the development of African Independent Churches, which practiced Western beliefs but maintained African practices deemed key and vital for African cultural survival. The new churches promoted and maintained polygamy, women circumcision, drum beating, traditional dressing, all forbidden in Christian (missionary) churches.

HOW EUROPEANS TREATED THE AFRICANS

For the Christian churches the differences between the two races were evident. The Africans and Whites had different sitting positions. Whites sat at the front section while Africans sat behind or on any seat not reserved for the missionary. The members were expected to dress in a certain style, not like the heathen. It was funny how an African was expected to wear a suit and a tie but with no shoes or how they carried bibles which they could not read. They learnt hymns which praised the White's culture and undermined the African culture. Sometimes the Africans just obeyed and followed what was preached or told without any basic understanding of the reason underlying a particular issue or practice. When questioned most missionaries or even Europeans responded by saying, "because God has ordered or it was evil." This practice and behavior cannot be explained better than it has been done by Colin M. Turnbull in his Book *The Lonely African* (1962). The author shows the confusion which faced many Africans who obeyed what was taught without any understanding. He observes:

> Masoudi was a good-looking boy. He was bright and cheerful and willing to learn the ways of the *Msungu* or white man .... And it was because he was good-looking the same account went, that Masoudi was asked by the *Bwana Mkumbwa*, the administrator, to become his

houseboy at Maladi. The villagers were used to such things from the Arab slave traders, so they were not unduly surprised that the white man should have the same strange and, to them, rather ridiculous customs. They did not expect it to last long, and soon Masoudi would be back among them. At this school Masoudi was taught by the priest, before anything else, that he was evil, that he had committed the most unforgivable crimes even for a savage. He recalled how funny it had seemed to him that whitemen should call him a savage, when they were so plainly savages themselves. But anyway, he was taught that if he wanted to live forever .... he would have to say he was sorry for being evil, and that from now onwards he would trust and obey the greatest white man of all, someone who was evidently even greater than the king of the Belgian: *Bwana Yesu*. So, following the line of least resistance and not really understanding one bit of it, Masoudi became a Christian. There were certain annoying things about it. One of which was that when he tried to prove that he was not really like the animals savage .... he was told he must not even do that, for it also was evil. The mission eventually gave him up as one of their many failures .... The mission puzzled Masoudi too, because they would never explain anything. When he asked at the office of the administration why he had to do something, it was explained to him. But at the mission, when he asked why he could not sleep with girls they simply said that it was bad, and that *Bwana Yesu* has said it was bad (*Reprinted with permission of Simon and Schuster*).

AFRICANS' PROVE OF BEING HUMAN

In their effort to prove they were human beings and not savages or animals, many Africans tried to be highly educated. Some were even more educated than the Whites. Unfortunately, such education only made them speak the White man's language but did not give them jobs. Even when employed, their wages were still low as compared to those of other races. This practice was well spread all over Africa - where missionaries, settlers and traders were established. Manual workers who did not require any special skills were equally paid low wages. Various studies from Nigeria, Liberia and Kenya have shown that because African laborers were untrained and unskilled, they deserved low wage rates. It was also argued that the African ways of life did not need much cash to service. But the same African paid less wage was subject to several taxes. He had to pay head tax, school tuition for his children, hut tax, church due and animal tax. Added to these was his day-to-day requirements: food, shoes, bicycles, and clothes. With this kind of life, the African could not make ends meet and was bitter that the White man had come to his village. The traditional harmony of the society was no more. The Africans could be punished for not working hard, planting on time, keeping his compound clean or for failing to attend a meeting. Those appointed as supervisors were not better off. They were to serve as models of good behavior among the community members thus in case they failed, their punishment was severe. This made them bitter and resentful toward the White man's way. They treated their people as slaves. Whatever was right in their eyes was stupidity in the eyes of the White man. In this kind of atmosphere, tension between the two races was a mounting each day. This bitterness is expressed by Matungi, a villager from East Congo:

> I have tried hard to understand the white man and his ways, but I can only see harm. What happiness have they brought us? They have given us a road we did not need, a road that brings more and more foreigners and enemies into our midst, causing trouble, making our women unclean, forcing us to a way of life that is not ours, planting crops that we do not want, doing slave's work. At least the Ba Ngwana left us our beliefs, but the white man even wants to steal these from us. He sends us missions to destroy our beliefs and to teach our children to recite fine sounding words; but they are words we believe in anyway, most of them. According to our beliefs, which is more than the white man does (Turnbull, 1962 Used by permission *of Simon and Schurster*).

Another villager questioned their moral - family life of the White. He complained: "We have several wives, and we are faithful to them all, and we care for all their children until we die. You people cannot even be faithful to one wife, and your children are such a nuisance to you that you send them away from your house almost as soon as they walk" (Turnbull, 1962:28). Like this villager, given an opportunity many Africans could tell of their experiences with the Whites.

COLONIALISM AND THE SEGREGATION OF THE AFRICANS

Although apartheid was said to be confined only in South Africa, I believe the whole of Africa has experienced some form of apartheid. What is the difference between apartheid in South Africa and where the Whites could not mix with the Blacks? At times, to appear more polite, the Blacks and the Whites have had church services at different times. Even some places saw different buildings and different church leaders - Whites and Blacks separate. In hospitals, Africans could be treated outside while the Whites were attended in better places. Africans lived in villages while the Whites lived in spectacular buildings taking almost a quarter of an acre. While over a thousand Africans were confined on small pieces of land, individual Whites occupied hundreds of acres, sometimes, thousands. Exploring this issue further was Dr. Marion Forrester, an American Economist. In his study concerning the effects of urbanization to the Africans, Dr. Forrester noted that:

> The character of each nationality in blended into this virile city. The European live in houses surrounded by their beautiful traditional garden, and in their midst is set their Cathedral -- A building which might be found in any part of the English countryside. Most Europeans are in Government employment, or high grade employees in tertiary industry. The European shopkeeper class has grown but by no means so much as Indian consumers. The link with Britain, usually spoken of as 'home' even by Kenya - born Europeans, remain very strong. Most children receive their education in England and administrators usually return there on their retirement. The new roads reflect "home" by their names, Prince Elizabeth Way, Hurlingham Road, Mackenze Road and Victoria Street .... Africans are primarily settled in local houses, or in housing estates (estates meaning lord) accommodating 114,000 Africans' (1962:40).

LET US CIVILIZE THE HEATHENS

The Europeans thought the African needed to be civilized from his primitive and heathen practice and nature. In fact, all the colonial powers had one main goal, civilizing the Africans. Different methods were used to achieve this goal. For the French and the Portuguese, civilization meant "assimilation". The logic behind this move was based on the believe that the Africans had no civilization. The two powers also believed to have the supreme civilization in the world. As such, they wanted to civilize the Africans. This way they would save the Africans from savagery and primitivity. They wanted to have civilized Black Frenchmen and Black Portuguese to achieve this. Assimilation was to produce Blacks speaking, walking and reasoning like Frenchmen or Portuguese. These Blacks attained "better privileges". For instance, they were to be given French or Portuguese citizenship and were to be subjected to French or Portuguese laws. They could vote and be voted for in parliament in Paris or any other administrative positions either in the colonies or in France. Those who failed to attain the level of assimilation set were still subjected to colonial rules. That is, they could not vote or be voted for and remained victims of oppression.

The Portuguese even replaced all African names with Portuguese origin names. By so doing, the African were expected to be cut completely from their culture, belief, past and social harmony. However, the African culture was rich and difficult to replace overnight. It was a culture which had developed or evolved over centuries and people were deeply rooted in it. This meant the French and Portuguese could not achieve their goal that easily.

With much frustrations, both colonizers gave up the practice. The French did this in 1920 while the Portuguese did so in 1961. They discovered that their so called "superior" culture was a failure and could not be forced on the Africans. The result was frustration and humiliation. As for the Africans, they knew what their belief was. They took from the French and Portuguese what was desirable but left anything that was worthless. As the saying goes among French speaking African countries, "assimilate but do not be assimilated." That is, take what is worth from the French culture but be careful not to be taken by the French culture. This was a good policy among Africans which challenged the French to know that they dealt with more than savages.

The African reaction did not however, make them more human in the colonizers eyes. In fact, the African did not need to prove who he was to the Europeans who had judged him as inferior and good only for work. From all angles an African was oppressed and exploited. It is noteworthy to point out that of all colonies in Africa, the Portuguese were the most brutal and cruel exploiters. In his book, *Emergent African States: Topics In Twentieth Century African History* (1976), the author S.A. Akintoye has given three main reasons why the Portuguese behaved this way.

The first was due to the Portuguese traditions of colonial rule. From the sixteenth to the ninetieth century, the Portuguese used their coastal possessions as sources of slaves for the Atlantic trade. During those centuries, too, the Portuguese kings used to reward their families and friends with large colonial areas and sent military expeditions to help conquer such estates over which the Portuguese owners then exercised almost unlimited power. When Portugal had built an African empire after the scramble, these former colonial practices were continued in modified forms. For instance, forced labor become more than a modern version of slavery. Also, just as the Portuguese kings used to grant large colonial lands to individual noblemen, modern Portuguese government granted large colonial lands to European companies and gave them almost total sovereignty over such lands.

The second factor was due to the poverty of Portugal her self. With no capital to invest in the colonies to develop their economies, and little or no manufactured goods to import in exchange for their raw materials, Portugal found that their easiest way to derive wealth was to exploit the labor of her colonial subjects. This was done using forced labor which was virtually unpaid for.

The third reason for Portuguese repressive rule was the type of government under which Portugal itself ruled from the 1930s. Portugal became a republic in 1910, but because the Republican government achieved little or no economic progress, the army seized power in 1926. Finally in 1933, Dr. Antonio de Oliveira Salazar became a dictator promising the people of Portugal great economic achievements. Salazar seized all power in his hands, abolished civil liberties and turned Portugal into a ruthless police state and extended the same rule to the Portuguese colonies. It was a major part of Salazar's program to use the colonies to rebuild Portugal economically and to give the Portuguese a feeling of national greatness. In 1968, when Salazar became too old and too ill to continue to rule, he was replaced by Professor Marallo Caetano, who promised to continue Salazar colonial policies and he did so until 1974 (pp. 41-42).

In this kind of environment, the Africans were to suffer through hard labor and torture. Even before this time, during the peak of slave trade, the Portuguese regarded and treated Africans as less human. In the Portuguese definition of an African, he was referred to as an indigenous. This meant he was uncivilized and was subject to all Portuguese laws in relation to the natives. For instance, he had to:

1. Carry an identification always or else be imprisoned for a term of corrective labor (hard labor);
2. Get permission to look for work;
3. His children were forbidden to attend state schools;
4. Get permission to visit any foreign country apart from South Africa and Rhodesia;
5. Get permission to slaughter, sell or give away his animals; and,
6. Get permission to withdraw money from his bank account (Akintoye 1978:43)

Even where jobs existed, the Portuguese natives had first priority, even when they were illiterate and unskilled. The Africans remained uncivilized and without human rights. Only when they were assimilated could they be termed as human. They could be given identity cards. To qualify, an African was required to speak Portuguese language, to be able to earn enough money to support himself and his family, be able to "possess" the qualities and social status deemed necessary for a Portuguese citizen, must not have run away from Portuguese army, and must in general be regarded by the Portuguese officials as a "civilized' man of good characters and acceptable habits" (Akintoye, 1976:43).

DO NOT ASSIMILATE US

Although many Africans could qualify to be assimilado (term used for those assimilated) few ever applied for it. While most felt the process of attaining such status was too frustrating and humiliating. They also hated the status. Becoming an assimilado did not make an African totally equal to a Portuguese irrespective of his education. Even when given a job, an assimilado was still paid less. He was also subject to heavier taxes than before. One final humiliation to the Africans was the fact that being an assimilado meant losing his African identity.

He was not entitled to anything considered African. For example, he could not inherit his father's or relative's property or be a leader in the community. This discouraged many Africans who preferred to remain poor and oppressed than losing cultural identity. It was better to be called a savage or uncivilized but still be rooted to the community, the source of life.

NOAH'S CURSE ON AFRICANS

Outside Africa, the same story of uncivilized Africa was well spread. Both America and Europe saw Africa as a dark continent. It was a continent where savages, jungles, chaos, witchcraft, and other evil practices existed. Tracing what could be some of the sources of such negative attitude towards Africans, the author of *Africa: The People of an Emerging Continent*, Sanford J. Unger has noted that:

> The puritans made much of the negative connotations of the dark skin, and they were among the first to invoke biblical support for theories of black inferiority, including such devices as Noah's curse. Then the ideas arose about African's closeness to the "natural life" their similarity to apes and other dark animals, their tendency towards promiscuous sex and other sins (1989:22).

This and many other stories made Africans looked like real animals in the eyes of other continents. According to Melville Herskovits, an American anthropologist .... "Africa's people were held to have fallen behind in the march of progress, with ways of life representing early stages in the evolution of human civilizations" (p. 22).

AFRICA: UNSUITABLE FOR HUMAN SURVIVAL?

Many reasons have been given in relationship to current state of an African and why he remains uncivilized. Some scholars and observers have associated the whole issue with climate which was termed to be unsuitable for human survival. Expressing this point further, in his article in the March 1910 issue of the *Atlantic Monthly*, James M. Habbard noted:

> With the exception of a small tract of the East coast, it is land in which no white man can live for any length of

> time and retain his faculties in a normal condition. There
> can be no doubt that much of the misgovernment of the
> Congo native is due to the terrible influence upon the
> Belgium official of the climate and   the unnatural
> surroundings. More than one traveler has called attention
> to the fact that some of the officials in the isolated
> stationsare practically insane (in Unger 1989:22).

But this observation did not hinder the Whites from coming to settle
in Africa. For over fifty years, their population had increased
dramatically.   Most came as settlers and settled in the Africans
highlands which were said to be cool and suitable for their settlements.
In fact James Habbard was right when he concluded that although the
continent was unsuitable for survival, in thirty years of the civilization
Europe will have poured into the barbarism of Africa. In his view,
Habbard saw the need for the Africans controlling their own continent
just like the Whites controlled theirs (p. 22). But his view was not
supported by majority of the White people who saw great prosperity in
Africa.   Commenting on how the Whites were to occupy and
eventually settle in Africa, Samuel Phillips Verner, a missionary
explorer from Alabama, U.S.A., concluded in the *Forums*:

> It is interesting to consider the exact means by which the
> white control and direction of Africa will be carried out ....
> The fact that Africa is to be a white man's land is now a
> forgone conclusion .... the high, mountainous, healthy and
> invigorating parts of Africa are on the slopes of the
> mountain ranges and on the watersheds of the great rivers;
> these regions being distributed all over the continent,
> instead of being massed together in any one part. In these
> regions the Caucasian can live and labor. From them he
> will govern and direct all the rest (p.22).

And Verner was right. From the African beautiful mountainous
highlands and watersheds, the Whites operated and directed how
African resources were to be messed and exploited for Europe's
benefit. Were it not for the Africans who rose against this behavior
and the poor state of economy in Europe after the second world war,
those people would still be in Africa. If Africans were less human,
one would wonder how they could have organized themselves to get
rid of the White man from their land.   To the Africans, the land used
by the Whites had just be passed to them temporary. But the Whites

had a different idea. Having given some papers and coins (money in their culture), they thought to have bought the land that belonged to the community both the living those already gone to the world of spirits (living - deads). The land was treated with care and respect lest the mother nature become disappointed and refuse to produce good harvests. On the other hand, the White man having "bought" the land from the Africans, he could now afford to force them out of their land to squatter areas and keep "his" land for himself. He failed to understand the deep cultural rituals attached to the land and the relationship between those living and ancestors. Taking their land was like stealing, an abomination to the society which could not be tolerated. It is because of this belief and conflict of interest that the White man was to face strong opposition from the Africans. To them, they may have been cheated by welcoming the "strangers" but could not be deceived to give up their God-given possession.

> .... To fight for it, yes, and let the stronger win; there was no shame in that but to be tricked out of one's land, to be forced to give it up for all time without fighting, that was a disgrace difficult to live down (Turnbull 1962).

In his reaction, the White man explained to the Kikuyu of central Kenya that he took away their land because the tradition al methods of farming were not productive. In response, the Kikuyu demanded to be taught better methods of farming but were denied. The Whites took acres of land which was unused. The Kikuyu saw in this a strategy of taking the best of their land and keeping it. This was a bitter pill which none of them would swallow. It was this bitterness that led to the Mau Mau rebellion against the Whites. A war that continued till independence when the Kikuyu got back their lands. From then, the African in Kenya and elsewhere learnt a lesson. He learnt that his honesty in thought and action could betray him. He also learnt that not all that shone was diamond.

It would appear the Whites were genuine when they told the Africans that they wanted to take care of their land. However, their goal was to civilize them. Unfortunately, civilization was to take only the form designed by the White man. A less human creature could not be given full status of a man, meaning the White man. According to Major Fredrick Russell Barham, a pioneer in the Boy Scout Movement, in his book of tales from Africa. "It would be as insane to give (Africans) a smattering of our involved religions belief and so-called education as it would be to give our children sticks of dynamite with which to play." To him, an African could not be considered capable of accommodating what the White man possessed in terms of beliefs and knowledge. However, he gave a solution to the Africans: "only as the Black's skull grows thinner and their brain heavier will they absorb our ways and standards .... At present they are at the stage of development equal to that of children eight or ten years old" (In Anger 1989: 22-23).

To an African, Barham's comment is not only a disgrace but is an insult to his mental faculties and dignity. But Barham was not alone. Leo Forbenious, in his definition of a discovery in a West African tomb said it was "strange and mysterious .... delicious". But when it came to giving it credit he noted, as for the style and content, it was "typically African trash" (p.23).

WHY AN AFRICAN IS UNCIVILIZED

Nowhere in the world was an African ever recognized as a human being of normal capacity. He was in fact abused and mocked whenever he sought recognition for himself or for his children. In the United States, Black Americans (now known as Afro-Americans), once slaves obtained from Africa, faced similar hatred as seen elsewhere in the world. One such incidence was when they demanded for equal intellectual justification in resistance to integration of their public schools. The opposition to this kind of recognition was strong. In his opinion Henry Garret, once the head of department of Psychology of Columbia University, noted:

> ... over the past 5000 years, the history of Black Africa is
> blank. How could Black children study along side whites
> .... Where Black Africans had no written language, no
> numerals, no calendar or system of measurement. He did
> not devise a plough or wheel, nor did he .... built nothing
> more complex than mud hut or thatched stockade (In
> Unger 1989:23-24).

The opinion of Henry Garret which was published by Patrick Henry Press of Richmond, underscored the rich African culture, religion, social and political sophistication and peaceful harmony among Africans. Being ethnocentric he could not see anything good in the Africans. I am sure he had the same opinion for Asian communities, American Indians and other non-white societies. But Henry Garret did carry the whole burden of hatred and negative stereotypes towards the Afro-Americans (Blacks). To make sure the American society was poisoned from adults to children, Helen Bamerman, an English writer living in India wrote a book entitled *The Story of Little Black Sambo* in 1898. The book which was targeted to White school kids described the Black kids as lazy, slow and stupid. The kid was however said to be loyal to his White master but was liable to lie and steal and could do incalculable harm. This book remained in the standard American lists of recommended children books until the late 1960's (In Unger 1989:24). For over 60 years, the book was used in American schools besides its expressing views that an African could not be trusted or relied on. The laziness, slowness and stupidity of the African kid was of course related to his poorly developed brain. His system of thinking could not make him think straight. And because he was not able to think for himself, he relied on others to think, work and create for him. His roots were evil by origin and his relationship with spirits proved just this. How could he worship ancestors and the living dead? How could he offer sacrifices? How could he wear animal skins and not see himself naked? How could he raid his fellow neighbors and kill them? And above all, how could such a person claim to be equal to a White man? A person who lives in good modern houses, who grows beautiful flowers around his premises and speaks a language next to that of God. After all, the devil is "black", and his ways are evil, thus, condemnation to eternal hell. An African being Black shows how closely related he is to the devil and his evil behavior. The White man is clean and "free" from evil. His ways are truthful and his judgment right. As was explained to the Africans, the White man was expected to redeem and civilize the Black man to be nearly human though not equal to the White man. Under all circumstances, he will ever remain less-human no matter the methods used to civilize him. He will remain Black and Black is evil. And how can evil dwell with light? This was an illusion that had become an accepted *fact*

CHAPTER TWO

AN AFRICAN IS A HUMAN BEING AND COMPETENT

I think it is Africa, where man probably began, that can give men hope of a new life. By an immense combined effort Africa can save itself and given time, a vital breathing space, to the rest of the world. Even more, I believe, example to the older world .... (G.E.W. Wolstenholme in Man and Africa, 1965).

INTRODUCTION

The argument presented in chapter one has demonstrated the biases of the West towards the African person. The opinions and views presented have been carried over centuries since the West encountered the Black man. Stories ranging from evolution to biblical have been used to justify the arguments. In many cases the Black man has been treated as an animal capable of hard-work and nothing more. He the White man's wealth. The results being that the West has enriched and boosted its economy on the basis of the Africa's resources. To the African, the fate of discrimination, oppression and exploitation has resulted a devastating situation. The poverty, hard life and unpredictable future have their roots on the biases exercised toward a Black man.

Although Africa belongs to the black people by virtue of habitation and origin, the Black Africans live like refugees in their own land. Decisions concerning social, political and economy of their states rest at the hands of the West. Decisions not related to Africa have been imposed on the continent's people like young children. The authoritative approach of the West toward Africa has not only shown how dictatorial the West can be, but has at times proved the in human decent of the West. The African states have been conditioned before receiving any "foreign aid." They have been forced to submit to terms which are only beneficial to those giving aid. Resources which enriched Europe and America were removed from Africa. It is this same resources that are now siphoned to Africa as aid and Africans are expected to beg and acknowledge the giver as a "helper" rather than as an exploiter. It is like a father who sends a wife and children away. On maturing the father comes back to the children to be acknowledged as their father. The West exploited Africa and now want to be acknowledged as the god of the continent whose assistance is vital for human survival. The goal is still to prove to the African person that he cannot afford to do anything constructive by himself. He cannot manage the existing resources: land, people and environment. How can you blame someone of not being rich when you have already planned for his raid and he has lost everything? The West raided Africa and `stole' all that was worth. But now the blame is on the poor African who has no more than remnants.

I am not trying to say an African is a super human being than the West, all I am saying is that the approach of the West towards the African people is another method of showing an African how useless or less human he is. He is not capable of managing his own affairs or manage his own house. The question is whether an African is less human as has been advocated. Is he really that damn not to know what is going on? Where did all this idea of being less human came from? Why was the African the victim of such abuse and not another race? Is there some truth in all the accusations?

The answers to these questions are the bases of this chapter. The chapter explores the views of the West toward the Africans and their origin. It also aims at digging deeper to the truth or false associated with these theories. The chapter hopes to leave no stone unturned that needs to. If by so doing we can clear the ground for our future generations and cooperation between the Whites and the Blacks, both within Africa and without. Through proper understanding of the

Africa man, we can respect, recognized and uplift him from his oppressed and exploited state. His children and wives can have some where to live in the world and at least be being respected as human and as worth living.

THE AFRICAN WORLD

For centuries, African people remained closed to the rest of the world. They carried their daily activities without any concern for the world outside their worldview. To them, the world was what surrounded them. Beyond their world was a world of strangers - people who needed to be treated with care and suspiciousness. Each community operated and did that which concerned it. Frequent clashes between tribes or ethnic groups was common but this did not worry the communities. It was away of life. The communities though they could fight often, they still relied on each other for food and other trades. Barter trade was common and each community traded what it lacked. And there was trust on what was traded. The communities had different but similar rituals. Such rituals were related to worship, offerings, confession for societal sins and passage from one age group to the next. For example, passage from childhood to adulthood through circumcision.

While Africa maintained a peaceful life, the rest of the world was undergoing great changes. In Europe the industrial revolution was gaining momentum, meaning Europe needed more resources for its industries. The urge to explore and acquire new states and protectorate was growing among European nations. During the whole of 19th century, Europeans presence was felt in all parts of the world. The British had already made their presence in India, Africa and East Indies. The Dutch had taken their role in South Africa as far back as the 17th century.

THE EUROPEAN IMPERIALISM AND SUPERIORITY

By the 1880s and 1890s, the Europeans administration was well established to be able to plan, set up colonial governments and run efficiently. Imperialism was becoming a reality for many European states, a thing which they could not imagine or thought of centuries before. With much confidence, Europeans started to see themselves as superior people. Looking around them, they saw the material products of the industrial age -- railways, cheap cotton, textiles, telegraphs, iron ore, ships -- a product of their brains and intelligence. Their states gross national products (GNP) grew heavily as compared to the rest of the world. They saw themselves not only as human, but as special species.

In their book, *African History* (1988), the author Philip Curtin, Steven Feierman Leonard Thompson and Jan Vanshan have observed that in this kind of position for the Europeans: "It was only natural to reassess their position in the world, to increase the value set on their own culture while simultaneously lowering their estimation of others" (pp.449).

It is note worth to recognize that for centuries, the Europeans had a negative attitude towards other races. In the authors' opinions:

> Africans were perhaps 'lower' still, since they had long since entered the fringes of European society overseas through the slave trade, Asians, from Turkey to Japan, were thought of as barbarian heathen, though here dislike was sometimes wiggled with respect for Asian power or admiration for Asian products such as Chereses porcelain and Indian fabrics. But even that respect tended to diminish in the nineteenth century, as the Europeans saw themselves far ahead and increasing their lead in all things technological (pp.449-450 Used by Permission *of Addison Wesley Longman*).

But industrial development was not the only reason for Europeans looking down upon other races. In the early nineteenth century, new current in biology made them evaluate their position. Their thought and trends were strongly influenced by the assumption that the natural order of the universe was a "great chain of being"? This assumption was based on Plato's views of intelligence. The assumption implied that:

> ... all created things would fit into hierarchies of values - in biology for examples, into phyla ranging from the higher animals to the lower, a classification system still used today. As biologist of the late eighteenth century became concerned with the place of humankind, it seemed natural to classify *Homo Sapiens* as the highest animal. It was also natural to expect the varieties of mankind to fit into a similar hierarchy from highest to lowest. Because the classifier were Europeans, it was

equally natural to place the European variety at the top, and to grade others downward from there. Skin color is the most obvious physical difference. Since the biologists automatically placed the people with pinkish - yellow skins like their own at the top, they found it easy to place the tropical Africans with their dark brown skins near the bottom - and this arrangement had the virtue of conforming to the existing social states of `black' and `white' on the American plantations. It also followed in the eyes of these biologists, that the superiority of the `higher races' was part of the natural order of things, that it governed their intelligences, their aptitudes and capabilities, hence their `natural' role in history; and the same was true of the `lowest races' (p. 450 Used by Permission *of Addison Wesley Longman*).

The Europeans' pride and superiority complex promoted racial hierarchies and maintained them on top for a long time. The Africans, American Indians, and the Asians had come to believe what was preached as a virtue. They considered themselves as the lower beings. Unfortunately, however, the classification did not continue forever. This was doomed when scientific doctrines of racial inequality were proved wrong. Although Europeans took it for granted that physical appearance was a mark of the deepest significance in determining man's dignity, this was scientifically opposed. But the effect of this opposition was not felt till late in the 1920s. But the prejudism continued as was witnessed during the ideology of Nazi massacre of the Jews community, a community considered as cursed.

RACIAL HIERARCHY

During the climax of the racial hierarchy, that is between 1880s and 1920s, Europe had the greatest impact on the world. In fact, it was during this period that Europe also conquered most of Africa. And it was the start of its opposition that European impact in Africa started to loss much meaning and later the African states, got their independence. It is important to note that Europeans' conquest of Africa was not merely because of pseudoscientific racism but to acquire the region for their material gains - industries. However, racism did have a profound influence on the way the colonies were administered and run. Most of the administrators still had the mentality of a `lower placed Blacks' when they entered Africa. It is this mentality that made them abuse the Africans and their continental resources.

Reacting to the idea of "higher" and "lower" classification as developed by Plato and later used by the Whites as a basis of grouping other races, Jacqueline Strain in her book *The Constitution of Ancient Greece* (1971) has warned that:

> The terms "higher" and "lower" are dangerous since they suggest a mere scale. It does not follows, because X makes Y more intelligible that it makes Y better. Unfortunately Plato constantly made this illegitimate influence. He also assumed that illumination always operates from general to particular. But actually there is no fixed order, or direction of illumination. Sometimes particulars are illuminated by generals. (Thus an abstract, dictionary definition of horse may be made real and significant by our becoming acquitted with some particular horse, with the pleasures of riding him, need of caring for him, and so on). What illuminates what in any given context depends on what we already know and what we want to know. But considerations like these takes us for beyond Plato's own formulation of the view (p. 201).

I agree with Strain. The judgment or classification done should depend on what we already know and what we want to know. When we classify races, what is it that we want to know about them and why do we want to classify them? Most of the past conclusions were based on prejudice rather than on logic. It is important to aim at knowing more that just merely judging from the surface, a judgment often used by those using higher and lower classification. An African was classified as the lowest in the hierarchy simply because of his color. If the Europeans did go deeper than the surface, they could have discovered an intelligent and respectful man. We should not stop at assumptions. We should aim at proving them to develop facts and principles which we can use and defend. As Strain concludes:

> Every science, then starts from certain assumptions. It must not forget that its starting point is only a set of assumptions and that study of them might radically alter the science's notion of itself (p. 202).

This is a wise observation to consider. Assumptions are never made facts before they are tested to see their viability and reality. This is a concept the Europeans forgot when they judged other races.

Without specifying racial differences, the author of the book, *Minor for Man: The relations of Anthropology to Modern Life,* Clyde Kluckholn has observed that "The characteristics of the human animal which make culture possible are the ability to learn, to communicate by a system of learned symbols, and to transmit learned behavior from generation to generation" (in Strain 1971: 25) without any discrimination to a particular race. Strain has explored how a child develops from infant to a capable individual, able to reason and take judgment. The process starts with the parental care which involves behavioral patterns development and intellectual growth. As conscience is strengthened within the individual, parental direct control diminishes. And "by the conclusion of this initial stage of the socialization process, the child has learned a number of those habits, values, and attitudes which together comprise the culture which each generation in every human society passes on to the next "(p. 29)

This is a profound finding which does not distinguish a White child from a Black child. The process of growth is the same - both socially and intellectually although the geographical factors may vary from one region to the next. It would be absolutely wrong to try and teach children of their superiority or of their inferiority complex. Such teachings are translated to behavior practices which promote hatred rather than understanding between races. An African would hate and dislike his European, Asian or Jewish counterpart on the basis of the understanding that they not only despise him but they do not regard him as human, a sad attitude which can be difficult to heal. This kind of behavior has been demonstrated in many African states. Upon getting independence, most Europeans left Africa because they could not entertain Black supremacy. They could not see how `slaves' and `third class-citizens' as Africans were referred to, could be of equal class to superiors. It is a practice that has repeated itself recently in South Africa when the country got its independence in 1994.

AFRICAN CIVILIZATION

It may be wrong to continue blaming the Europeans and other White people for regarding Africans as uncivilized if we can't show how Africa was civilized before the coming of outsiders to the continent. It is wise to explore briefly the history of African civilization in order to determine the sense of humanity or less humanity present or absent.

Our focus is specifically concerned with Africa South of the Sahara, a region long termed as uncivilized and as the dark continent. I would give much credit to the authors of *World civilizations,* 1986 (Seventh edition), Edward McNall Burns, Philip Lee Rajpa, Robert E, Lerner and Standish Meacham, for their great work. Their approach is well balanced and not based on racial differences. According to the authors, civilization in the Sub-saharan Africa was relatively slow as compared to other places like Japan, something well explained by geographical location of the region from the rest of the world. "The continent possessed few natural harbors, leaching of the soil's nutrients contributed to a general scarcity of good land, and the vast Sahara inhibited meaning for cultural and profitable commercial exchange. Desert transportation was dangerous and unreliable with horses or oxen" (1986: 344).

According to the authors, before 200 BC, most of the Africans South of the Sahara region functioned as nomadic hunters and food gatherers. Socially, the people were organized on the basis of kingship. Their leadership or authority was exercised by priests, rain makers and in some communities, elders. Religiously, this was based on superstition and remained animistic by nature. In this type of religion, ancestral worship was central. This gave the community a sense of continuity and guarded the society morally. Different rituals were performed to please and maintain healthy relationship with the ancestors. Intermediaries chosen among elders were given the responsibility of interpreting the will and messages from the ancestors and other gods. Population density was very low thus there was no need for centralized government. Also, the fact that there was no external threats show little need for organized military cadres for defense.

As far as their technological development was concerned, some Africans developed exceptionally advanced skills in metallurgy. For example, about 1500 years ago, Africans along the Western shore of Lake Victoria had developed a medium carbon steel in forced draft furnaces. In fact, this sophisticated technology to the world was not matched by Europeans for centuries. Also of great consequence "was the smelting of iron for the production of spears and hoes" (p. 344)

The Africans had known about iron for along time. In fact, some isolated sites of iron age go back as far the Sixth century BC Examples of such sites were in Northern Ghana, Nigeria, Ethiopia, and Northwest Tanzania. In Eastern Africa, regions along the great

158, 371

lakes and upper Nile were other sites. In West Africa, however, it is probable that iron-smelting techniques could have filtered across Sahara from the North Africa, especially Phoenician coasts. Before the end of the first century AD, the iron age had spread among the Bantu of Central Africa. This enabled the Bantu speakers to clear forests and to cultivate different types of food crops. The most notable were coco-yams, plantain, and bananas. The major tools used were iron hoes and machetes.

Increase in food production meant increased in population. This, by 200 AD population explosion among the Bantu made them to expand across the breath of the equatorial Africa. With much food, there was no need to migrate to gather food. This led to the establishment of village lives. Other trades also prospered. Of particular importance was barter trade where metallurgists bartered their finished goods like iron, ore, copper and salt. By the end of the tenth century, most African communities used iron tool and spoke Bantu languages. As the authors notes:

> . . . from the Cameroons to the South African veld they spoke Bantu - related languages. Bantu peoples has thus initiated an agricultural revolution and accelerated the development of new mechanism for social organization and control in East, Central and Southern Africa. In effect, they laid the necessary foundations for the civilizations which emerged in the millennium after 900 AD (p. 346).

Other forms of civilization took the form of introduction of iron technology in West Africa by the Nubians of the upper Nile and Sahara Berbers; introduction of the camel in the trans-saharan trade. This was well established and widely used by 750 AD. Also there was the Awkar Accrue. The Negro Berber state was located in the South-Eastern area of the present day Mauritania. It acted as a middle position between the gold miners from the southern forest and the Berbers traders from the North. By the eighth century, "the 'Ghana', or king .... and his people were known in North Africa and the Middle East as the world's major gold export" (p. 346). The Arabs soon invaded North Africa and traded for Sahara salt. By about 800 AD, the trade between Arabs and Berbers traders had spread all over Western and Northern Africa with trade routes reaching upper Niger River, Morocco, Algeria, Tunis, Tripolis and Egypt. In Eastern Africa, the Arabs and Bantus also traded and by 900 AD, intermarriages between the Bantus, Arab, Shirazi and Indian families had started. This led to dynasties and organization of formal seaborne trade which was facilitated by Monsoon winds (p. 344 - 348).

The internal African trade and civilization was later to be disrupted by Europeans' invasion of Africa beginning with the Portuguese in Eastern African during Sixteenth Century.

With this type of development in Africa, Africa although termed by the Whites as the dark continent, it was only dark to the Whites, not the Arabs or Indians who had traded with Africans for centuries. It was also the Whites view that the Africans were inferior, but what they lacked was a comprehensive understanding of Africa and its people, something which made them judge Africans wrongly. It would be wrong to assume that the Europeans brought civilization to Africans. From Europeans' history, it is clear that civilization originated with Sumerians and Egyptians. What they forget is that Egyptians are Africans.

HOW DOES A NATION BECOME CIVILIZED?

In concluding this chapter, it would probably be wise to ask ourselves, when does a nation becomes civilized?. According to Henry Muoria, the author of *The Gikuyu and the White Fury*, 1991:

> It follows, when we asks the question as to how a nation becomes civilized, the answer is that it happens when it acquires the knowledge of writing its own affairs, when it learns how to build permanent houses and beautiful ones at that, when it learns how to make steel instruments and how to use them and when it acquires the ability to investigate the best way in which it could increase its knowledge (p.172 Used by permission of *East African Educational Publishers Ltd.*).

It follows then, Africans knew how to write, (Egyptians), how to build permanent houses and how to work with iron long before the Europeans' invasion of the continent. It shows how intelligent they were and are. They may have taken long to develop their technology, but it was their innovation and invention. This prove their being equal if not above other races in knowledge and wisdom.

Reacting to the Whites accusation of inequality and inferiority of an African, in his first speech on arrival from Europe, the late Mzee Jomo Kenyatta, Kenyan first president noted:

> My friends, since I left this country of ours, I have visited a lot of countries of Europe. And I have learned a lot of things. Above all, I had ample time to study very closely the brains of all human beings on earth, that is to say, those of the Europeans, Chinese, Indians, and Africans. I can tell you they are the same, but where the difference occurs is in the use is these brains. Nations which have made great progress, and those nations which have failed to use brains, have remained behind. And that is what we Africans have been doing. If a mother of a child bind its hand as soon as it is born, that hand will remain like that and the child will never be able to use it. And if a man fails to use his brains in his life, they will never be of any use to him .... (1994: 17 Used by permission of East African Educational Pub. Ltd).

Mzee Jomo Kenyatta further observed that what an African needs is more integrity and be honest at heart. "And above all, we must realize that there is nothing that is done by White men which cannot be done by us Africans if we are united (p.17).

Mzee Kenyatta knew the danger of dishonesty and division of societies and the harm that can results. But this issue of lack of unity was soon to be realized. This came during the struggle for independence in Kenya. The Europeans made sure that the unity among tribes was minimal. They especially opposed any effort by Kikuyu (biggest tribe in Kenya) against uniting with other tribes. The tribe was thought to be very intelligent and educated, causing threat to the Europeans' presence in Kenya. Reacting to this behavior, Kenyatta argued:

> There is a certain Gikuyu (Kikuyu) proverb that asserts: `A hypocrite does not like another hypocrite; he prefers the company of a fool to whom he could lie easily'. So when we follow the teaching behind that proverb, we are to understand why the White people hate the Gikuyu more than any other tribe in Kenya. The White men are given to thinking very deeply about knowledge or scientific methods, you can study all kinds of things and objects from the smallest to the biggest ones like the stars and even you can arrange or marshal such knowledge in a

manner that would enable you to know that, when such and such things are mixed together, the result is such and such. To gain knowledge by that method is known as experimenting with things and objects under study. One could study animals and their behavior until one could say, if you do this and that to an animal, the animal would do this and that .....yet, there is one kind of animal, which they have not been able to investigate so closely and so understand it thoroughly like everything else that happens to be subjected to such scientific study to know all their secrets such as the trees of the jungle .... This means that man is a special creature by God in a mysterious way. And that is why it has not been possible for his inner secrets to be known in a manner that would enable another human being to know exactly what the other man is thinking about even though he is created in the same way as the scientific investigator himself. There are a number of reasons which serve as good evidence to prove that the white man does not like the Gikuyu tribe at all, for instance, their failure to be employed as soldiers in the white man's army. While other Kenyan tribes are employed as soldiers in great numbers, the Gikuyu are very few .... But why should that be the case? If we were to think a bit hard, we may discover that the Gikuyu by nature are given to asking questions or to wanting to know the reason why as a habit.... (That sort of attitude is contrary to the White man's traditions of fighting solders, which is expressed in their saying: 'yours is not to reason why, but to do or die' which means ordinary soldiers are expected to obey orders of their superiors without asking why such orders have been issued in the first place) (pp. 159-160 Used by Permission *of East African Educational Publishers Ltd.*).

THE UNBIASED EUROPEANS AND AMERICANS

The behavior illustrated above shows the European practices all over the continent where they established themselves. But it would be wrong to judge all Europeans or White as against Africa and terming the Africans as inferior. There are many cases of Europeans and Americans who have fought for an African identity as an equal human being. These people value human beings. These people value human races as equal and deserving all due respect as God's creation. I have many White friends who love and care for the Africans. Their concern for an African society is that of commitment and devotion. Many have spent years in African as missionaries, doctors, expatriates and friends. They reflect Dr. David Livingstone's spirit when he set for Africa and spent his whole life serving and evangelizing Africa. His love and great commitment can only be expressed by his own words in a speech delivered in England during his first visit after being in Africa for several years:

> If you knew the satisfaction of performing a duty as well as the gratitude to God which the missionary must always feel in being chosen for so noble and sacred a calling, you would have no hesitation in embracing it. For my own part I have never ceased to rejoice that God had appointed me to such an office. People talk of the sacrifice I have made in spending so much of my life in Africa. Can that be called a sacrifice which simply paid back as a small part of a great debt owing to our God, which we can never repay? ... Anxiety, sickness, suffering or danger now and then, with a foregoing of the common convencious and charities of this life may make us pause and cause the spirit to waver, and the soul to sink; but let this only be for a moment. All these are nothing when compared with the glory which shall hereafter be revealed in and for us. I never made a sacrifice of this, we ought not to talk when we remember the great sacrifice which he made who left his Father's throne on high to give himself for us 'who being the brightness of that Father's glory, and the express image of this person, and upholding all things by the word of this power, when he had himself purged our sins, sat down on the right hand of the majesty on high' ... I beg to direct your attention to Africa; I know that in a few years. I shall be cut off on that country which is now open; do not let it be shut again! I go back to Africa to make an open path for commerce and Christianity; do you carry out the work which I have began. I LEAVE IT WITH YOU! (Worcester. Ir. PP. 56-57).

The call by Dr. Livingstone was positive and successful. Many missionaries, explorers and traders came to Africa. Thanks to those who had the same clean spirit as Dr. Livingstone. World leaders have also carried strong campaign against racial differences especially among the Blacks, both in Africa and outside Africa. Among them is the late President John Kennedy of the United States. Recognizing the dignity of an African, in his address to the American Society of

African Culture in June 1959, Kennedy said that Africa is "a land of rich variety of noble and ancient culture ..... of vital and gifted people," He was especially against the late president Nixon's statement that U.S should be "winning the battle for men's minds" in Africa. In Kennedy's view, " ... the people of African are more interested in development than they are in doctrine. They are more interested in achieving adecent standard of living than in following the standards of either East or West" (Unger 1989: 60)

To show his commitment to Africa, Kennedy proposed the establishment of an Educational Development Fund for Africa by the United States. It is said that during his 1960 campaign and speeches, Kennedy made 479 references to Africa. And in his approach and positive attitude towards Africa, Kennedy succeeded in changing American policy for Africa. Between the last year of the Eisenhower administration and the first year of Kennedy's reign, total economic assistance to Africa more than doubled to reach $459.9 million. Allocation of "Food for Peace", and aid and financing guaranteed by the export-import also increased and by 1962, Kennedy increased military aid to Africa (p. 60)

During Kennedy's years in the office, twenty six African presidents and prime ministers visited him in the White House. And through governmental and private programs, potential   African leaders and thousands of students went to the United State, some of them remaining there for years (p. 61)

CONCLUSION

Many leaders of the world have come to change their people's attitude about Africa. It has been recognized that an African is no longer the monkey like creature still in the state of evolution but is just like any other human being. This makes him equal to a White man or other races on earth. No longer higher class, lower or higher faculty, no superior or inferior. All human beings are the same regardless of their geographical or social background. And so are the Africans.

CHAPTER THREE

ARE AFRICANS TO BLAME FOR AFRICAN CRISIS?

Africa is passing through such terrible times that the question is not survival. The future remains unclear. We are being cheerful to say that should things continue as they are only eight or nine African countries out of 50 OAU members could still survive a few years from now (Edden Kodjo, Secretary General, OAU, April, Lagos 1980 - cited by Obi Bini, "OAU Holds Conference" Guardian - May 28, 1980, p.15).

INTRODUCTION

Crisis in Africa has reached a level where it cannot be ignored any longer. The past three decades have witnessed an extremely unbearable situations in many African countries. Although most of the countries hoped independence would bring prosperity and great progress, the opposite has resulted. Instead of progress and prosperity, most countries have experienced under-development and widespread poverty. It is even wrong to call Africa a developing continent while it bears all qualities and characteristics of an absolute under-developed nation or state. As economists and other policy makers have classified some countries as under-developed, most African countries are considered less developing. In actual fact, however, it would be right to classify most of the countries South of the Sahara as not only less developing but worse, that is, they are developing backward.

Probably before deciding whether Africa is developing or not, it would be wise to look at some of the characteristics of a developing nation. For a country to be considered developing, it should reflect the following factors.

1. There should be a multidimensional process in the whole structure. The process involves significant changes in social, political and economical structures.

2. There should be signs of attitude change both from social point of view and institutions.

3. There should be an increase in economic growth. This means, an increase in the Gross National Product (GNP) or state's wealth.

4. There should be positive trend toward reduction of inequality in income distribution, and,

5. There should be positive move toward eradication of absolute poverty (Tedaro 1994).

The goal of these signals or symbolic characteristics aim at restructuring the whole social and economic system with the sole purpose of attaining better standard of living for all.   Unfortunately, most countries in Africa show no sign of development. Most still lag behind in development with their GNP declining annually despite their increase in population and dependence on the West. The countries still bear the characteristics of less developing countries with no sign of ever improving.   Nearly all the countries are still agrarian in nature, with one or two cash crops as sole source of income and foreign currency. This dependence on agriculture makes it difficult to plan effectively as most of the products produced are nature dependent. Most crops depend on rain which is not always available at the right time. Research has shown that two out of five years are drought years and farmers usually lose most of their crops during this period.

INCOME INEQUALITY

Due to poverty spread as a result of income distribution inequalities, most people given a chance accumulate all the wealth they can. This promotes selfishness and greed for wealth, whether from state or public organizations. But this does not reduce poverty by any chance. To the contrary, the poor continue to increase at an alarming rate because only the rich persons have access to any means of wealth or resources. The poor are left uncared for although those in government preach the common tune that development is for all, rich and poor. It is a tune that has caused more tension than harmony in the countries. While the poor interpret the tune as mocking, the rich use the opportunity to justify their wealth. While most poor persons promise prosperity for their counterparts should they gain power, they usually forget their lame promises as soon as they achieve what they wanted. And within a few years, they cannot be distinguished from their so called "enemies" before they got into power. And so, the poor person is left without hope of ever recovering from his God forsaken state.

With the rich remaining rich and the poor remaining poor, the gap widens apart. With governments solely depending on exports of their few crops, the market is out of the governments' control. The West still maintain the capability to measure and determine what is to be presented in the market from Africa. This means the governments of Africa have no power of deciding how much their products will sell. This also makes it difficult for the governments to plan for their people.

LEADERSHIP STYLES

A major characteristic of the countries is that of leadership. With tension existing between the rich and the poor, a means of control to maintain peace and harmony is developed. For most countries, the mean is authoritarian leadership. Few people from the governments sometimes run the countries with the help of military officers or armed forces. The government is the instrument for peace because once it is put down, chaos and massacre arise from those considering themselves oppressed.

The state of African countries South of the Sahara still remains a mystery to the world. It is not clear why the region has not shown signs of development. At least that is how someone from another continent will reason, but not from Africa.

THE LOCATION OF THE AFRICAN CONTINENT

All sorts of stories, myths, and folk tales have been developed aimed at showing that the Africans are to blame for the crisis existing in their continent. Although Africa is the second largest continent after Asia, and although it has the richest number of resources which are yet to be tapped, Africa remains the poorest and least developed in the world. The question as to why this is the case remain to be answered.

Most people have not blamed the Africans for the crisis in the continents. Most blame nature for the location of the continent on the face of the earth. Africa is the only continent which the Equator passes in the middle. This makes the sun to have a direct effect on the agricultural crops planted. In case the rain fails, the sun burns all crops, the only source of food and income for majority of the populations.

Stories and myths have explained that an African is a lazy and unproductive person. Other stories still maintain that an African is not careful enough to take care of what God has given him. Still others feel an African is not capable of managing African resources. Africans are termed as poor managers and careless when it comes to accountability.

There are many stories to further the criticism of the recklessness of the Africans, thus leading to the African crisis. The state of Africa is deteriorating every day, from social structure of the people to natural beasts and environment.

In an article entitled "The Vanishing Herds" appearing in *Food Monitor* (May - June, 1978:23), the author A. Dobrin pitied the African beast which he considered as dying at an alarming rate, a blame he associated with expanded farming:

> The last of the world's greatest herds are dying. East Africa's primitive Savannah country is shrinking as the land comes under farmers' ploughs. Thus are the herds

> vanishing, pushed from their natural grounds. Within the
> foreseeable future, the glory of the primeval migration
> across Africa's plains will be gone forever ....

The danger to wildlife will mean a reduction of the countries'
tourism attraction business, a source of foreign currency and leading
industry for some countries South of the Sahara. This will mean lack
of employment for those employed in the industry which in turn will
mean a decline in living standard.

FOOD PRODUCTION VERSUS EXPORTS

Although people in Africa may be starving due to lack of food, there
is evidence that the countries could feed themselves if only they
concentrate on food production rather than on exports. A look at
most states will reveal that much of the best agricultural land,
traditionally used to grow subsistence food is now used to grow
export crops. As the people become hungry each day and wild animals
are pushed further and further into some marginal areas, the countries
continue to increase their foreign-currency earning crops. Thousands
of acres are used to grow coffee, tea, cotton, rubber, pineapples and
groundnuts for export to Europe, Germany, England, Austria,
Belgium, France, among others. It is not uncommon to have a
plantation of pineapples surrounded by slums of hungry poor Africans
who have never tasted the fruits. They are enjoyed by those abroad
and those who can afford to pay more. The governments have been
blamed for not taking care of their own people. But remember the
same countries that blame the African governments are still the same
that initiated the plantations for their own goals and benefits.

Analysts feel that the real problem in most countries South of the
Sahara is not lack of food. The real problem is policy makers. While
they make decisions to set aside thousands of acres for cash crops,
very little land is set aside for food stuff. In fact, most countries have
enough productive farmland to feed all their people and still leave
room for wild animals and natural forests.

The argument is that, if African governments were to make more
balanced economic and agricultural policies, the problems of food and
wild animal threats would be no more. Yet the countries have made
little effort toward this end. It is another cause of blame on facilitating
crisis in Africa.

With no strong policy on land usage apart from those used for cash crops, most of Africa's land continues to become a desert. According to *Wealth and Poverty: An Economic History of the Twentieth Century*, (1990), in the 1970s and 1980s, deserts were made to grow larger. Apart from climatic change, the problem was associated with population increase and new technology. Practices like over-cropping and the reduction of fallow periods exhausted the top soil making it poorer and subject to heavy wind or rains leading to erosion. Similarly, desertification was said to be as a result of overgrazing and the collection of wood especially on pasture and shrub land (p. 222).

Concerning famine, the report noted that in 1977, a conference on desertification had come down in favor of numerous projects which were designed to reverse and control desert advancement. The projects were based on knowledge gained in the West on similar deserts. However, by 1984, the United Nations Environmental Program (UNEP) reported that only one of the projects had been realized. Unfortunately, some $10 billion had already been spent between 1978 and 1983 on infrastructure and preparation but virtually nothing was spent on desert itself (p. 222). Of course, the problems goes to those meant to implement the projects. They were supposed to monitor them to ensure that money was spent on rightful projects rather than different projects. A good look at such practices show lack of good insight for the future. Desert is of a more threat than the infrastructure problem, a problem that the implementors did not see.

DESERTIFICATION

The problem of desertification is evident in most African countries South of the Sahara. Rain failure leading to prolonged drought has led to great famine in most countries. The world is caught up in the web of not knowing who to blame, nature or African governments. But the situation does not get better, but worsen yearly. Before 1983 and 1984 drought which made matters worse in Africa, about a fifth of Africa's people relied on imported grain. It is sad but true that Africa seems to be losing the battle to feed itself. The number of people under malnutrition and hunger is on the increase. The situation although worsening seems not to worry the international community or the African governments, otherwise, they would do something to alter the situation. It is only when there is a cry for food that the governments run to seek for food aid. As soon as hunger is over, the problem is forgotten. No long-lasting solution has been established nor being worked out. Programs like soil-conservation, tree planting, good farming methods are only given emphasis in only few countries, for example, Kenya. This short sightedness of most governments rather than long-range planning have made most African governments not to plan effectively. No wonder, the problems in Africa have worsened.

With an increase in population, expansion in deserts, deteriorating standard of living for the majority of African population, sub-Sahara Africa experienced a weakening economic performance during the 1970s and 1980s. The situation has gotten worse during the early years of the 1990s. The economic blow has taken the forms of decline in per capita income for most countries. As usual, rapid population growth was associated with the poor performance. However, weak economic management was said to be the major contributing factor to the crisis. The effect was poor investment, poor health care and deteriorating educational level in most countries.

Realizing the worsening situations, most governments in Africa have started to re-evaluate their policies in order to improve. At the United Nations (UN) Special Session on Africa in 1986, the governments "submitted a Program of Action for African Economic Recovery and Development." The program recognized the failure of past policies and stressed the need for sustained reforms (*World Development Report*, 1988:28). The success of such reforms will and does depends on the governments' commitment. This may vary from one government to another.

THE POPULATION EXPLOSION THREAT

I have mentioned population increase as one of the crisis in Africa. It is strange how Africa was able to sustain itself during the 1970, but today it is on the world queue for food begging. By 1984, those requiring foreign imported grain totaled 140 million people, a figure that has increased in present years. Strongly held traditional beliefs have been associated with increase in population. In many communities, children are still considered as source of wealth or security. Women are still seen as assets for child bearing rather than as love companions. A man without children is considered unfortunate and useless. In such cases, the brothers or friends often bring up children with the man's wife to cover his embarrassment. Similarly, if a wife fails to get children, the husband marries another woman.

On average, an African woman has eight children although this figure is declining due to strong family planning campaigns. But the campaigns are still less effective especially where they contradict traditional beliefs or religious practices. The Catholic church, for example, has been singled out as a key opponent to medical practices on family planning. Most Africans support the church thus making it difficult for the governments to succeed. With increase in population, food needs expand.

This in turn leads to severe soil erosion, a problem of virtually every African country. According to a 1978 report the problem is becoming critical. The report puts it in a graphical language:

> An environmental nightmare unfolding before our eyes ....
> a result of the acts of millions of Ethiopians struggling for
> survival: scratching the surface of eroded land and ending
> further, cutting down the trees for warmth and soil and
> the country denuded .... Over one billion - one billion -
> tons of top soil flow down Ethiopian highlands each year.
> (Source: US Agency For International Development,
> "Fiscal Year 1980 Budget Proposed for Ethiopia",
> Washington, DC 1978)

As population continues to increase, more soil goes to the sea, more forests disappear, and deserts expansion become a reality. It seems the governments have given up their efforts to control the worsening situation. But one thing is clear however, without better methods of agricultural control and family planning methods, the countries cannot expect miracles to increase their per capita food production.

The world should not be concerned with population increase only as a source of problems in Africa. I think there is more to the problem than population threat. For example, while the governments have focused on population as the sole threat, they have forgotten their role of administration. The farmers have not been taught good methods of farming to increase food production.

As a result, although per capita grain production peaked in 1967, it has been declining by nearly 1 percent annually. The decline has been attributed to three interrelated factors, a) the fastest population growth in history, b) widespread soil erosion, and 3) desertification. Increase in population leads to demand for cultivation land and clearing of forest which in turn expose the top soil to erosion. Erosion leads to removal of top soil. The result is unproductive land, semi-arid or desert. The chain seems evident everywhere in Africa. According to "USDA, Economic Research Service (ERS)", 1950 - 1983, (1984), the bottom line of the problem stems from the failure by African governments to give agriculture the support that is needed. This shows that if the governments play a significant role in agricultural development, food production would be high, population would not be a threat, soil conservation methods would be effective, and desertification would not be a problem. As for now, the poor farmer has to make his soil produce more to meet his needs. Unfortunately, what was produced last year cannot be produced this year. Yield per acre declines annually, yet population increases at an even faster rate. He cannot fail to see crisis continuing and his life worsening. As he cries to the government, he knows the answer would be, "reduce your population." Without the know-how, his efforts only brings another life to the desperate world - the world of poverty.

DROUGHT IN AFRICA

Although nature is often blamed by man, Africa seems to experience prolonged drought as a result of man's interference with nature. However, it is sometimes difficult to verify facts on the issues. Long before the issue of population and over population became a focus of development, Africa still experienced great droughts. In fact, it is almost impossible to draw a line of demarcation between human effort and natural effects. This makes it hard to judge whether man is solely responsible for crisis in Africa or nature. A look at the continent shows a great fluctuation of climate. According to National Research Council, Board on Science and Technology for International development, a reconstructed climatic history of the Sahel over the last 10,000 years demonstrates extreme fluctuation, from periods of wetness to dryness. The Sahel region has experienced a periodical deviation of severe prolonged drought. And early this century, the drought of 1911 and 1914 was so severe that it reduced the annual discharge of the River Nile by 35 percent. Similarly, the drought reduced the depth of Lake Chad by 50 percent. Most rivers and lakes levels fell during this period. And the trend has been repeated throughout the century (1983). The drought of 1983 - 1984 saw not only rivers drying, but also most rivers falling in levels. Most rivers are yet to regain their original levels. Lakes especially along the Great Rift Valley have suffered greatly from drought. Some like Lake Nakuru and Lake Elementaita are examples of lakes threatened with drying up should drought continue.

CIVIL WARS

But the African problems do not end with drought. Civil wars from all corners of Africa are creating more harm to the already devastated population. Angola, Mozambique, Uganda, Somali and Liberia, are just few examples where war has caused more suffering in the last three decades. By 1992, 20 wars had been fought in Africa since 1960. The result has been death of 7 million people while 5 million turned into refugees, not to mention billions of dollars in destruction and havoc on struggling economies (*African Report*, May - June 1992:40).

It is sad that a continent faced with food, economic, social and political crisis still spend million of dollars on arms. Rather than spends money to educate or improve the standard of living for its communities, most governments spend money on arming themselves against possible future aggressions. As a result, Africa spends $14 billion a year on arms. This is equal to expenditures on education and four times health spending. This figure may vary from country to country. For example, Ethiopia alone spent $10 billions on arms imports from the former Soviet Union during the 1980s. And according to United Nations study report, both direct and indirect costs of 10 years war in Southern Africa, that is, Angola, Mozambique and Namibia was $60 billion (*African Report*, May-June 1992:40). This money if well spent could have raised the standard of living for inhabitants in these countries.

But the war meant more suffering for the poor Africans. In Somali, inter-ethnic conflicts left 30,000 people dead in 1992 and over a million refugees in a matter of weeks (p.42). Yet most of these wars are instigated from within - tribal differences, power struggles, corruption and material greed. The effort of Rwanda government to eradicate and finally kill one tribe led to over a million dead in 1994, a horrifying situation to the world. It is a situation which can be repeated anywhere in Africa. Unfortunately, instead of solving the crisis themselves, the warring parties usually invite outsiders to mediate peace among them. But usually, there is mistrust as to the sincerity of the mediating parties. This makes such peace-making efforts frustrating. Most of the mediators are former colonial powers. It is ironical how African states refuse to solve matters in Africa and go to the mother colonizers as peace mediators. It is easier to hold a meeting in Portugal, Brussels, Britain or Washington rather than meet in Nairobi, Cairo, Harare, Lagos, Cape Town, Addis Ababa or Accra.

It shows how Africans trust is limited toward their fellow Africans or neighbors, a cause for further conflict

ENVIRONMENTAL DESTRUCTION

According to FAO, the extent of environmental destruction is more severe in Africa than has ever been seen elsewhere. Overall, some 3.7 million hectares of forests and woodland disappear annually. For example, in West Africa, 4 percent of its dense forest is cleared each year. The harm is further extended to the trees that are scattered among farms and pastured areas. The problem is made worse by increase in population which means more and more bush is cleared to give room for cultivation or to give room for extra herds of livestock. The method weakens the top cover leaving it open and subject to erosion and strong winds. From this form of exposure, Africa is said to lose between 20 to 50 tones of top soil every year from cultivated areas. The United Nations Environmental Programme estimates that a total of 742 million hectares or "more than a quarter of the whole continent is in the process of becoming useless for cultivation" (Harrison 1987:27). The reports notes that as a result, the continent is undergoing severe or moderate desertification. The danger to this process is evident. That is:

> ... deforestation and soil erosion are undermining the very resources on which Africa farmers and their families depend. Africa's environmental crisis will deepen and perpetuate her food, poverty and financial crisis. It threatens not just the hope of progress, but even the hope of survival (in Harrison 1987: 26 - 27)

THE EFFECTS OF POVERTY

Between 1960 and 1965, the first half decade of development after independence, the average rate of growth of per capita real gross domestic product (GDP) in Africa was 1.4 per annum. This figure was the lowest in the world. In fact, Africa even lagged behind average growth for all under-developed countries which maintained 2.3% per annum in the same period. Similarly, there was a decline in the average rate of growth of annual Gross National Product (GNP) in the period from 1950 to late 1960. Thus 1950-1955, 3.9%; 1955-1960, 4.2% and 1960, 3.6%.

The consequences of low productivity in agriculture has led to deteriorating social life-style for most people in Africa. The effect is poor health condition for most people especially those in rural and slum areas.

According to nutritionists, the average daily intake for a healthy life is at least 2500 calories. But in Africa, majority of the people have intake that is below this figure. Children are also said to be faced with the problem of protein deficiency making their growth slower and weaker bodies compared to their counter parts in the West. Increased decline in agriculture productivity is associated with this trend. One of the main reasons for the decline has been replacement of traditional crops with cash crops. In some areas there has been a shift from grain or yam production to the cultivation of cassava. The problem with this type of change is that the new crops planted may be very low in protein content. In other places, cash crops like coffee, tea, cocoa, cashewnuts, and cotton have made it impossible for farmers to grow non-export food crops. The matter is even made worse by the governments that restrict any reduction in cash crop occupied lands.

Other problems of poor health are related to the high incidence of disease. From children to adult, health problems exist. Research reveals that infant mortality is 50% higher in sub-Sahara Africa compared to anywhere else in the developed world. Children are greatly hit by Kwashiorkor. Either, Africans are victims of low resistance to other epidemics. The leading killer diseases are: Malaria, Pneumonia and Cholera. Water borne diseases, for example, parasitic diseases are common. Hookworm and schistosomiasis are some examples. While these diseases are as a result of poor supply of clean water, the problem is associated with inadequate hospital facilities and poor management especially on the part of government agencies. Instead of using most medical facilities to help the public, most government officials use them for individual gain, private clinics or selling them at a profit to private hospitals.

AFRICA'S ECONOMIC PERFORMANCE

Since independence, disappointed by their economic performance and political systems, majority of the countries are suffering from an uncertainty and badly focused future. While most started the 1960s with great hope of progress, the hope has turned to hopelessness. Most are uncertain of their future and as they look forward to some form of mystery development, they cannot tell where they want to be ten years from now.

And there is a cause for concern for the countries. Looking at the trend of development in the African countries, the vastness of the crisis is apparent. Toward this analysis, some facts are worth noting.

1. Sub-Sahara Africa per capita income dropped to about 0.4% per year in real term during the 1970s.

2. Per capita food production is declining; for instance, in 1983, this was only 79% of the 1961 - 1965 average and the per capita GNP in 1984 was 12% below the 1980 level.

3. Food imports have continued to increase between 1961 and 1983, food imports have increased from about 8% to 23% of all cereal requirements.

4. Population growth is on the increase. The growth rate stands at 3.1%. This is up from 2.3% in 1960 (Odhiambo et al. 1988:21-22).

The changes have not been matched with any development as such. Increase in food importation reflects a danger of declining agricultural productivity and fast rate of population growth. However, production decline in the continent is also experienced in other sectors of the economy. Two major areas of concerns, have been mining and industries. In 1982, mining output was 68% of its 1970 level while most industries operated at 20% to 40% capacity due to extreme scarcity of imported spare parts. There was also scarcity in factor inputs (p.22). And because Africa greatly depends on the three sectors - agriculture, mining and small industries, the economic and social life have been affected adversely. As a result, unemployment, under-employment and absolute poverty have increased. The human life is thus characterized by hunger, malnutrition, and reduced life-span. Human survival has become a matter of luck rather than a right.

Efforts to solve the crisis in Africa have been minimal and only applicable during emergency situations. For example, during famines, massive food aid is available from the international community but after the matter is brought under control, Africa is forgotten. No long-term economic or social solutions are developed. The African governments usually appear desperate or irresponsive toward solving the problems. The reaction has often led to lack of interest among donor countries who may be dismayed by the behavior. Sometimes fed up with the whole ill-treatment on their part by the African governments, donors often abandon their missions of assisting Africans. In many cases they accuse the governments of interfering with their goal due to corruption, threats to donor's activities, dictatorship, and violating human rights. In response, international community may decide to employ its machinery to protect the donors from governments' interference. There are times when United Nations has even employed its forces to ensure the poor African get his basic need; food, shelter and protection, which his government threatens. It is ironical that African governments should be protecting their people, and not the outsiders. This indicates lack of direction on the part of the governments. A reason why most people would rise against the governments with the goal of changing them.

THE FISCAL DEFICITS

Another approach to Africa's measure of economic problem concerns the rate of growing fiscal deficits, inflation and shrinking of the money economy. According to the editors of *Hope Born Out of Despair, Managing The African Crisis,* Thomas Odhiambo, Professor Anyang' Nyong'o, Emmanuel Hansen, Godfrey Lardner and Dustain Wai:

> ... the external accounts of many countries in the regions show widening current account deficits, declining net capital flows, negative reserves and mounting arrears on debt service payments. Indeed, as most African governments have sought finance from outside to contend with growing balance of payment deficits, the twin spectres of indebtedness and yearly rising interest have emerged (p. 23).

The problem of debt is worsening in Africa. However, compared to other developing countries Africa may not be considered badly off. By 1988 when the debt was $200 billion, the continent accounted only 10% of the developing countries' debt. But the ironical part of it is that the burden debt service obligations takes between 50% and 60% of export earnings (p.23).

The problem of debts seems to be getting worse annually. Over the past decade, the debt grew at the rate of 22% per year. Unfortunately the capacity to pay the debt declined due to decline output and export. As a result, only half of the current debt is being serviced on time. Although most countries have tried to reschedule their debts, this has not eased the crisis. The rescheduling rarely solves the real causes of the problem. That is, "remedial actions are attempted without coming to terms with the fundamental structural problems" (p. 23). Unless the countries come up with new methods of servicing their debts, it is impossible for them to satisfy their creditors for future help. But this may not be an easy matter to solve. With the current crisis in Africa, it would appear very difficult to come up with ever-lasting solutions. With difficulties in environmental control, population increase, low agricultural output, poor medical facilities coped with overall poor management, Africa is at the bleak of unlimited needs with few solutions or alternatives to offer.

EDUCATION SYSTEMS

The system of education has been blamed as a root cause of most problems in Africa. The African governments have been accused of spending too much on arms and "white elephant" projects than on education. As a result, most of the existing crisis could be traced to low level of education in the continent.

Research shows that Africa has the highest illiteracy rate in the world. By 1970, the number of illiterate aged 15 and above was 139 million. The figure rose to 156 million a decade later. The majority of illiterate group were women. The reasons could be associated with strongly held beliefs that girls should not be educated as they are considered to be assets of their parents (source of wealth during weddings).

Even for those countries where education has been emphasized, the quality of education has progressively deteriorated. Many institutions of education - primary, secondary and universities - have failed to produce quality graduates. The problem is attributed to lack of educational facilities, lack of qualified teachers and inappropriate system of education. This has caused frustration to the graduates and humiliation to the governments which have to admit their failure. The education is no longer seen as a way of breaking the intellectual bondage of colonialism. It is no longer the chief means of creating the appropriate skills necessary to advance economic growth. In fact, although education has drained most governments finances, it has been a disappointment to many.

The blame on education has become associated with the discipline chosen. For example, the humanities related education inherited from the colonial powers have done little to bring positive change to the economy. In many countries, technical and scientific education have been neglected for the last three decades. The effect is lack of enough personnel in the field of agriculture, medicine and industrial sectors. Most governments have started to re-shape their systems by giving much attention to technical education. Unfortunately, the students who are faced with the challenge find it difficult to acquire new skills having been trained only on humanities. As a result, governments have invested too much funds in the systems but little progress and benefits have been realized.

Even when the governments have continued to modify their educational systems, the approach has shown less positive signs. This is frustrating to the countries because even the institutions of high learning are not enough to produce qualified personnel needed to manage the complex economy, social and political systems. As of now, there is a confusion as to the best systems of education, how much to invest to bring change and what level of investment is worth to alter events in Africa.

POOR PLANNING

Planning is essential for any sector or country that intends to achieve certain objectives or goals. Planning is the process of establishing goals or objectives to be met on a future date, short-run or long time period. This is key because it enables one to decide whether the expected course of action was realized effectively or not. It is important to plan whether for small or big institutions. This means states are not exemptional when it comes to planning. A good plan for a country means prosperity and development in all sectors of development.

The African governments have been accused of having done a poor job of planning thus the current crisis. Upon independence, the governments' machineries were expected to control and manage the overall economies. This meant that all economic and social decisions were the work of the states. While this approach could have been effective if well facilitated, it proved to be ineffective. As a result, many governments have found it difficult and costly to maintain the whole economy using the approach. There has been incidents of misuse of funds and mismanagement of state corporations and parastatals enterprises. Many policy makers have even questioned the importance of such institutions as state owned or controlled. It would thus be important to explore why the states decided to take and run such agencies. There are several factors associated with their creations:

1   After independence, the nationalist governments wanted to gain control of their national economies.

2   The private sector was, and still is, largely foreign-owned in many African countries. This meant the absence of an indigenous capitalist class made it easier for an inordinate expansion of parastatal enterprises.

3.   African leaders felt that parastatals would be useful agents for economic development for their countries.

4.   Public corporations were considered to have advantages over the inherited colonial civil service because the public corporations would be more flexible and potentially in a position to contribute to national capital information.

5.   Public enterprises, would, in the view of these African nationalists, take on the role played by African entrepreneurs in other countries. This was expected to help harness, mobilize and exploit resources which would otherwise lie idle or be developed only by foreigners. It was hoped that profits generated by public sectors (parastatals) would accrue to the state and thus be available for public investments and for fostering the social welfare goals of the government (Odhiambo et al. 1988:26).

The above objectives appeared noble for the public sectors' creation. However, a look at their performance show that the approach was probably not well facilitated or it was a wrong approach all together. It would be wise to examine the whole establishments in the right of it effectiveness. This is important because most of them have become burdens to the states. They have also incurred great and enormous financial disabilities thus draining the already starved economies. Unfortunately, governments still continue to invest more and more funds in hope to make them productive. This has only worsened their performance. Instead of becoming source of income/revenue for the states, they have become parasites.

CONCLUSION

In conclusion, African problems are considered to be African created rather than Western origin or mothered. The overall poor performance of national economies have been attributed to poor management, poor agricultural methods, increase in population, poor education system, bad management of debts, poor planning and short-sightedness of national governments. The effects have been low productivity, unemployment, hunger, high infant mortality and wide spread poverty. The effects are greatly felt in the sub-Sahara region, a region where life appears bleak and doomed for current and future generations.

CHAPTER FOUR

THE WEST IS TO BLAME FOR UNDER-DEVELOPMENT IN AFRICA

The essence of Neo-colonialism is that the state which is subject to it is, in theory, independent and has the outward trappings of international sovereignty. In reality its economic system and thus its political policy 4 is directed from outside (Kwame Nkurumah 1968 p. ix)

INTRODUCTION

With rich extensive resources yet to be explored, Africa is potentially the richest continent in the world. But Africa's riches do not seem to play a positive role in its development because compared to other continents, it is the least developed and the poorest. It lags behind all developing countries -- Latin America and Southern Asia. It is behind in food production, manufacturing industries and trade. Technically, the continent shows little progress. Africa's debt crisis is worse than of any other continent. Its people are among the poorest in the world standard and poverty strikes 90 percent of the continent's inhabitants. The African future is not expected to be different from its past three decades since independence. It is most probable that the present generation expects a worse life situation in the future compared to their parents, yet little is being done to alter the situation.

The current pathetic situation in Africa has been attributed to colonial governments. These authorities are said to have changed the social political and economical structure of the continent. The effects of colonialism are far reaching as seen in Africa today. In fact, colonialism bears much blame for current African problems. It is worth noting that colonialism was wherever disruptive and destructive. The system disrupted and destroyed the traditional societies, economies and affected most established authorities.

The purpose of this chapter is to explore and examine the argument that the West is to blame for under-development and exploitation of Africa. The analysis is important considering that confusion may arise as to who is to blame for the African crisis, the Africans or the Westerners. The last chapter has placed the blame on the Africans. To balance both sides of the coin, it is important to examine the Europeans or the Westerners role in Africa and associated effects.

THE COLONIAL RULE IN AFRICA

The role of the European colonial rule in Africa had far reaching effects on the political structure of the continent. The plan to divide Africa was first done on paper at Berlin in 1884. However, it was not the paper partition that brought much problems but the implementation of the plan. As the plan was being drawn to share Africa, the Africans were not considered. This meant the powers catered for their own individual interests. The key practitioners of the 1884 conference were Britain, France, German, Portugal, Belgium, Italy and Spain. These states needed to establish their own areas of influence in order to be recognized by other states through the established borders. The effect of implementing the plan was the founding of colonies and protectorates. With superior weapons, the Europeans defeated the Africans who resisted. The defeat resulted because Africans had inferior weapons and also failed to unite against their common enemies.

The result of the defeat was that the African kingdoms, communities, and empires lost their rights and freedom to control what they previously owned. But the colonizers did not stop there. The French and the Portuguese totally destroyed the African states by the decisions made on how the states were to be governed, or how to manage traditional resources and economies. They ensured that national unity and national loyalty among Africans were discouraged. To them, the Africans were all the same although divided into tribal societies. They took advantage of rival tribes to facilitate their divide and rule policy. In this way they ensured that no national unity was possible. In case of suspected attempts by local tribes to unite, such efforts were crushed or crippled. They fought against any independent movements and encouraged other tribes not to join the opposing groups. This was a method of maintaining hostilities among tribes who were taught to hate their neighbors. The Africans were shown the evils associated with opposition of the White man. They encouraged suspicion among tribal groups in order to check revolts.

When the Africans learnt the truth about their colonizers, uprisings from most countries began. Unfortunately, independence did not bring individual tribes together. In real sense, tribes that were traditional enemies were sometimes brought together because the Europeans drew the borders for their own benefit. Both major and small tribes were divided - some were put in one country and the others in another. For example, the Luos of Uganda and Kenya were one group living around Lake Victoria. The Ewes were split into two, one group in Ghana and another group in Togo. The Yorubas were divided between Nigeria and Benin, while the Maasai were divided between Kenya and Tanzania. This explains many conflicts along the borders between traditional enemies or collaboration between similar and friendly tribes to undermine their national governments. It is a crisis which exists today.

Explorers, missionaries and traders played a key role of changing Africa. They particularly convinced their mother countries of the importance of investing their efforts in Africa. The response of their mother countries was that of supporting their agents in Africa in an attempts to civilize Africa, for their benefit. They set administration posts all over Africa as points of operation. For the French and Portuguese, their method of civilization meant assimilation. That is, the Africans were to be totally transformed from their black savagery and barbarism to Black French or Portuguese men. An African had to speak the colonizer's language, behave like a French or Portuguese to prove he was civilized. He could then graduate as a citizen of the colonizer thereby getting all privileges including those of voting or becoming an administrator.

THE COLONIAL TYPE OF EDUCATION

The Europeans did not only influence   Africa politically.   Their education is said to have had the worst effect in African history.   In fact Africa has not been able to free herself from the   effect.   Today Africa has taken the education as a virtue and all   Africans have to attain this education or else they will be   termed as underdeveloped.

On the whole, the European type of education has resulted in a very significant social and cultural change for the Africans. This education has produced a new class of people. The group speaks the European language, behaves like Europeans and tend to   think like Europeans. The result is a different type of African leaders, literate Africans. The group can travel all over the world and seems to be less in touch with their traditional cultures. In fact, Africa is in the process of getting a new culture - a culture that is not rooted in the African culture or in the European culture since the group is a master of none. Although   literacy has made it possible for Africans to put their traditional languages into writing thus making it possible for future preservation, most Africans have abandoned their languages in favor of the new languages. However, they have no alternatives since these languages are taught in schools and spoken in major gatherings and offices.   Not to speak English, French or Portuguese is to be uncivilized. To speak European languages is to be wise and intelligent. Using their exaggerated writings, paints, and pictures, the Europeans have considered   pre-colonial African as a jungle inhabited by barbarians and savages, members of the dark continent. The goal of the European education and culture was to bring light through civilizing the dark and backward   continent. With this goal, the European considered themselves to be gods, superior human beings. Nothing they did was questioned by the natives who were termed as less wise and inferior.   Instead of viewing colonialism as an oppression, the Africans were   made to see it as a God given opportunity which they took whole heatedly and honestly.

THE   SOCIAL-ECONOMIC   IMPLICATION   OF COLONIALISM

It is worth noting that the effect of the European influence was strongly felt in the urban areas than in rural Africa. Migration from rural to urban areas was also intense as the colonizers had brought a different method of earning money, working in industries in the cities. The pay was considered better compared to working in the rural areas and depending on subsistence crops and supplies. The resulting effect was strong migration to urban areas. This interfered with the traditional family structure. Instead of members of the family living together as they had done for generations, some members had to go to cities to look for jobs. In the cities, they lived alone or with few friends. This promoted individualism, a major characteristic of European societies.

Economically, Africa was not left untouched. The major mission of Europeans' coming to Africa was not civilization as they claimed, it was to exploit Africa resources -- its people and natural environment. Their purpose in educating an African was to make him a usable tool in the process of exploitation. If an African was given minimal education, he could supervise other African workers and he could read and understand instructions. Otherwise, if there was nothing to gain from an African, no colonial government would have invested its energy in the continent. The missionaries who brought the Gospel would definitely have spread the Gospel in Africa with minimal support from their governments.

THE COLONIAL GOVERNANCE-EXPLOITERS NOT DEVELOPERS

It is thus important seeing colonialism as an exploiter of resources in Africa rather than as a developer. During the eighty years of colonial rule in Africa, the colonizers left Africa with a mounting economic crisis that had never been experienced before. The crisis was a sign of their misrule and poor management. All economic activities were geared toward production of exports of agricultural raw materials to Europe. Once manufactured in Europe, the products could be shipped back to Africa where they were sold at high prices. The products were termed as "European Made" rather than "African Origin". And to promote the market, they taught the Africans to hate and dislike their own domestic products in favor of European made products. It was a psychological game of making the Africans slaves both physically and mentally. They succeeded to a great extent. Although they claimed civilization was their goal, the colonizers made little or no attempt to develop African economies to a level of self-sufficiency.

To make sure the Africans were not given any decision making power, the Europeans made all major decisions including terms of trade. They also fixed the prices of commodities exported to Europe. his was an effort to make Africans have no major knowledge of how to operate international trade which was left to the developed nations, Europe and North America. During crisis in Europe, Africa played the role of balancing the crisis. For example, during depression, Africa received low pay for her exports and in times of inflation, Africa had to pay more for imports from Europe and America. This way, the Africa's economy served the interest of the colonizers. To make sure the interest was served, Africans were encouraged to grow more and more cash crops - coffee, tea, sisal, cocoa, rubber, palm-oil and cotton. All these were then exported at cheaper prices but the finished products were imported at high prices. It was the Europeans' way of making Africa's wealth get to Europe cheaply and Europ's wealth to enter Africa expensively. So, Africa was boosting Europe's economies while draining its own.

Civilization or no civilization, Africa suffered during colonialism and continues to suffer today as a consequence of Europeans' involvement. As mentioned, during the Europeans' rule, cash crops and mineral mining were promoted and encouraged to serve Europe. Unfortunately, the opportunity cost of this practice was neglecting subsistence cultivation. Before the colonial era, Africa was self-reliant in food production. However, by 1950s it had become a key food importer. The Africans were spending too much time growing European market based crops that they had little time for growing domestic food crops. The Africans were forced to grow and spend all their efforts in plantations. Between the 1940s and 1950s, the effect of hunger among Africans was being felt. Many Africans started to migrate to urban areas in an attempt to escape from the worsening rural lives due to lack of food or to run away from forced cropping and forced labor. This made urban population unbearable and poverty among urban people became a matter of concern. The Europeans made no attempts to rectify the situation, and by the time they left Africa in the 1960s, they knew the mess they had caused. They knew the "African Man" had been destroyed socially, economically and politically.

Nothing done by Europe was meant to benefit Africa. Take the example of infrastructure, no major roads were constructed for Africa's development. Any major highway was only constructed when found to facilitate exports to Europe. Railways were constructed for the purpose of opening the African inland to European markets. Any place that did not benefit Europe lacked infrastructural development. As long as these roads, lakes and railways remained productive, they were maintained. As soon as they proved less productive, they were neglected. By the time the African countries got their independence, most of the roads and railways needed repairs. But without funds or good sources of capital, the African governments did not have the means to repair them. Today, most of the railways are as they were constructed during the colonial era with only minor changes, if any. The colonizers also did not make any attempt to promote internal development between countries or within a country. Where no benefits could be expected, the regions remained underdeveloped and resources untapped. Landlocked countries remained closed to the outside world and experienced little or no development.

Communication with the outside world using telegrams, letters, and telephones was confined to areas where Europeans were established. Even where such communication existed, it was controlled from Europe. It was and still is, more expensive to make a telephone call to an African country than to telephone a country in Europe. This is because telephones have to be connected through satellites controlled by European countries before the message is transmitted to the destined country. This is a relevant problem which continues to face Africa today.

When most African countries achieved their political independence, they expected great prosperity. This was demonstrated by the good prices that existed especially for Africa's cash crops and minerals. However, upon receiving their independence, their dreams were shattered. The countries' leadership lacked the expertise that was with their former masters. The former masters took advantage of this limited knowledge. The European economic experts convinced the African states to model their development programs to suit those of the industrialized nations - Europe and North America. In the book *History of Africa* (1989), the author Kevin Shillington saw the logic behind the European's approach as that of the relationship between the developed nations and under developed. The author notes: "The theory was simple: Europe was 'developed', Africa was 'underdeveloped' therefore, to rectify the problem, Africa must copy the European model of urban-centered industrialization"(p. 412)

Not really understanding the models used by Europeans, African leaders copied the models presented. By looking at how Europe was industrialized using the model, they thought this was a very appropriate way of making Africa achieve economic self-sufficiency.

Even though the European development took many years, they convinced the Africans that it was   possible to achieve quick development. To the Africans, "if   African countries were indus- trialized, then they could manufacture their own consumer goods which until then had been imported from Europe. This, in due course, would shift the 'adverse terms of trade' in Africa's favor and so halt the drain of Africa's wealth to the already 'developed world'" (p. 412). This was a great assumption which could not work. The European experts knew from their history that the model could not work for Africa. It did not work.

Similarly, the Africans were convinced that European technology was superior and could alter events in Africa. As a result, the African governments imported everything that seemed viable -- expertise, technology, building materials, machinery, education and health facilities. How were the governments to finance all the imports? It meant draining the existing resources - finance or borrowed loans. The practice worsened the matter because within a few years, the African governments incurred huge debts, with the developed countries. In order to clear these debts, Africa had to export heavily.   To ensure that the pattern continued, that is, Africa obtaining its imported resources from Europe and America, the Western powers made the terms of trade tough for the African's exports. The impact was that the African countries exported less at low prices while they imported more at higher prices. This led to a system whereby Europe and America dictated terms of trade and how Africa was to be managed.

Bitter with this practice and seeing how Africa had been deceived by the West, an African political leader and former Ghanaian president, Kwame Nkurumah termed the practice as 'Neo- colonialism' (1968:ix).   He was angry with Europe's continued economic control over politically independent Africa. He further observed that Africa claimed to be independent, but in practice, it remained a colony of the West. Unlike in the past when it served the interest of few individual countries, (colonizers), Africa served the interest of the whole of Europe and North America. Africa was in the process of becoming worse and it had been misled to believe that it was independent.

THE EFFECTS OF WRONG COLONIAL ADVISORY

Knowing what is meant to be developed and seeing that Africa was on the wrong track, a French economist summed up the issue by saying that Africa had made a "false start". As a result of much advice, Africa spent huge amounts of money in projects which resulted "white case elephants" across the continent. Several examples exist. Take the case of Akosambo Dam in Ghana. This project made Ghana incur a rippling international debt but had little practical benefits for the country. Although it provided sufficient electricity for Accra, it was to be insufficient in the future. By the 1980s, the Dam was greatly affected by drought that caused the fall of Lake Volta's depth to a level that the European experts had established for Dam's effectual operation (Mazrui and Tidy 1989:414). Another example is Zambia. After independence, the country had great reserves of copper. The country hoped to reap great fruits from the mining industry. This made Zambia give less attention to other industries especially to domestic agriculture. Zambia earned 92 percent of her foreign earnings from copper. It also composed of 53 percent of government total income. The effect of relying on this product was beneficial to European countries while the Zambians lacked food which the country had to import (p. 414-415) However, the blow came in the early 1970s when the copper prices collapsed and the country had no alternative but to rely on aid from the West, the same West that used her resources to enrich itself due to the poor advice given to the Zambian government.

The developed nations have used their strong position to exploit the poor African countries. When they export heavily to the West, the prices of their products are lowered, yet industrial products have relatively stable prices. Since 1960, Africa has seen its export prices on agricultural commodities drop more than ten or twenty times. Whereas African imports have continued to increase in prices, the fluctuation in prices of African commodities have made planing for the African economies difficult. The reliance on the Western dominated international market has made the situation even worse. Although Africa continues to produce more for the market, her gains have been minimal. For example, between 1954 and 1961, Africa's export to Europe increased by 75 percent. But due to falling prices, the total amount earned from exports by the countries only rose by 50 percent. The commodities exported also faced poor market as their prices fell. For products like coffee, cotton, cocoa, copper and tin, they saw a fall from peak period of 1950s to a severe slump by 1960 (Green and Seidman 1968:40). The problem did not stop at agricultural production but it also affected minerals. The fall in mineral prices was as a result of European's strategy to frustrate the industry. The European countries accumulated large stocks of minerals that their demand soon declined. Highly affected minerals were copper and tin. During the 1950s, principle buyers decided to buy huge stocks of the two products. By 1958, a country like Nigeria which exported the products in big quantities before, had its market fell by half. According to two prominent development economists:

> It has been estimated that the total loss of foreign exchange earnings to the African continent due to falling prices, particularly of agricultural products, exceeds all foreign funds which have been invested, loaned, or granted to Africa in the two decades since the second world war" (Green and Seidman 1968:39 - 40).

Faced with great needs for foreign goods and services, and with little purchasing power, the African countries have borrowed extensively from the West. The situation has led to increased debts to unmanageable levels. But the countries continue to borrow thus making them more subject to the Western decision making policies in relation to their exports. Institutions like World Bank and International Monetary Fund (IMF) have given Africa billions of dollars - loans in an effort to rectify the countries' economic situation. While the institutions could be seen as good samaritans, the opposite is true. Most development projects financed by them are concerned with increase in exports to off-set foreign debts. It is ironical how the institutions' objectives differ from that of helping the continent solve its problem although they appear to do so.

During the colonial period, Africa was made to concentrate on production of cash crops to be exported to Europe. Land that could be used for local food production was set aside for plantations. Big projects for irrigation to facilitate exports and European cash oriented products were encouraged. The practice was expected to change with the coming of independence. Unfortunately, the same trend has been maintained by local governments. The consequences has been poor prices of exports, hunger for the increasing population, degradation of soil and deforestation and wide spread poverty. This demonstrates that although Europeans left Africa physically, their presence has been felt indirectly. This has caused pain and much suffering for the continent. Since the trend does not seem to change soon or in the near future, Africa will continue to build the West while its walls are breaking down. Its people will continue to die of starvation while the West enjoys. While Africa searches for food everywhere, the West is wasting food everywhere. Also with worsening terms of trade, many African countries have shown a pattern of limited or stagnant economic prosperity. The problem has faced non-oil producing states. Compared to the period 1962 - 1972 when the average export rate was 6.5 percent, the average was only 6.8 percent between 1973 and 1977.

Analyzing the whole economy during 1962 and 1977, Africa experienced a relative decline in exports. The effect was a small contribution to the world trade. The slow growth of exports resulted from a fall in commodity prices in the world market and creation of protection measures in many industrial countries in order to control market. Without much power to voice their decisions, it was difficult for African countries to command any substantial level of the market. Unfortunately, the condition was worsened by increased prices of imports especially oil from OPEC countries. Imports from Europe were even tougher to acquire due to deliberate increases in prices (Mazrui and Tidy 1989:326).

THE COLONIAL POWER AND THE UNDERDEVELOPMENT OF AFRICA

Since colonial times, Africa cannot be said to be any better. The Europeans exploited her resources, its people and environment. What we see today has much to do with what Europeans started. How do we know that Europeans did not set pace for development in Africa? There are several indications to this. For example:

> 1) Africa remains the most under-developed continent among all third world nations. In 1976 statistics, Africa had 7.5 percent of world population. At the same time, Africa had only 2.1 percent of global GNP. 2) One claim by the Europeans is that they educated Africans -- civilization. Yet, by 1976, literacy stood at 74 percent. Asia had only 47 per cent while South America had only 24 percent literacy rate. 3) Also the Europeans claimed that they have improved the life-expectancy level in Africa. This can be refuted by comparing Africa with

other developing countries. The physical quality of life index has given Africa a figure of only 32, Asia 57, and Latin America 71. African countries are still behind of all Third World countries in areas like, infant mortality, public health, energy consumption and life expectancy (Mazrui & Tidy 1989:326).

The above observation reveals the true life in Africa. It is hard and tough. With about 54 countries, 16 of them are ranked as the world's least developed. That is, of the world's 25 least developed nations, 16 (64%) are in Africa. The countries are not only under-developed but they seem to be regressing backward. Most Africans have no hope of survival. Starvation and famine have shattered the hope of many. Parents are not sure they will see the maturity of their children. Children on the other hand continue to bury their parents on a daily basis. And while all this is happening, the West continue to demand for exports from Africa. After all, more deaths will reduce African population and she will be able Africa to export more.

The European's role in Africa lasted from 1900 to 1960 in most areas. For the Africans, this period is considered to be a humiliating period. Compared to other races, the Africans were second or third class citizens in their own land. The Europeans made sure they took the best land, occupied the best houses and took the best jobs. The Africans took the lowest paid jobs, lived in simple cheap houses and were confined to reserves and marginal lands. These lands were unproductive and desert stricken. The lack of productive areas to produce their own foods made the Africans to rely more on their masters for assistance. They worked on their masters' land in order to get their daily food and money; their pay was too little to sustain them and their families. To make sure the Africans followed the set standards and regulations, the Whites used the African chiefs and locally appointed administrators.

THE COLONIALISM DEBATE

Often, the question as to whether colonialism did develop Africa or not remains controversial in many ways. Some people have seen the African states as products of the Europeans' good work. This is proved when one looks at big cities; the Western cultural influence in Africa and 'improved' life standards. But critics have seen nothing positive from Europeans' occupation of Africa. It was colonialism with a purpose. The purpose was to enrich Europe through severe exploitation of Africa's resources. The Europeans' role completed the integration of the continent into a world system of trade and culture. This facilitated their penetration and occupation of African land. Africa was turned into a source of raw materials and a market for Europe made products. Different regions were known by the products they produced rather than by the inhabitants. For example, Ghana was known more for cocoa. Senegal was known for peanut production, Algeria for wine, Kenya for coffee, and Rhodesia (Zimbabwe) for tobacco. Ask the traders (Europeans) about the people who produced the products and the answer was obvious - Europeans. The Africans who did the manual work were not recognized and their contributions were insignificant. Before the coming of the Europeans, the African man never contributed anything to benefit the "world". His labor was valued in human terms, rather than on monetary ground. On the arrival of the Europeans, the African life was altered. Everything he did was valued in monetary terms. His sickness meant loss of his job, suffering of his family and leaving his master's premises. When looking for a job, he had to use a pass-book which indicated his previous employer, reason for leaving the job and whether he was recommendable for another job to another master. In short, he was a slave of his master.

It is argued that the European promoted regional development and unity among the African people. This they did by establishing new colonies and protectorates to replace African states and kingdoms. They brought different ethnic groups together and separated others using their official set boundaries. To them, the strategy could promote nationalism rather than tribalism. And to make sure the existing African groups ceases to exist, they gave each colony or protectorate a new national name, new capital city, a central government, official language and official system of governing. It was a way of setting a foundation for a future Africa, non-tribal and rootless society. But was this beneficial to the Africans or the Europeans? It was beneficial to the colonizers. They would never do anything that would benefit the Africans. Even saving a life could be done on condition that the life would benefit the master.

To form the colonies, the colonizers destroyed all existing states and kingdoms. They used force where the Africans resisted attempts to destroy the societies. Kingdom like Ghana, Mali, Old Oyo, and Songhai which were well established and united were totally destroyed. The traditional systems of governments and societal administration were replaced with organized machinery governments, centralized state affairs, judiciaries, civil services and armies. It was an effort to make sure the African people were revolutionized. That is, to make them abandon their beliefs, traditions, culture and religion. This way the Africans would be transformed from their old traditions to the Western culture.

How do we know the colonizers did not promote national unity as claimed? By putting together different tribes, others who were traditional rivals, this was a source of conflicts within the colonies. Conflicts that exist even today. Many tribal wars and rivalry have their origin from the time. Whenever the Africans tried to come together as a united group, the Europeans felt threatened. This is seen in situations where the Europeans fought, crushed and crippled liberation or independent movements. What they required from the Africans was not national unity but loyalty. They achieved this through different means. They got some African leaders, for instance, chiefs and made them collaborate with them. The chiefs and other administrators were supposed to preach the Gospel of loyalty and national commitment to the White man. The White man was superior, unquestionable and all-knowing. It was unheard to oppose one's master or Lord. However, this practice was not fully accepted by all Africans. Some rejected the White man from the beginning. He was seen as canning and evil person whose motive was to conquer and enslave Africans. To overcome such people, the Europeans used the tactics of divide and rule. Those loyal to the Europeans were favored and encouraged to remain peaceful. The loyal members were warned against the White man's rivals who were termed as enemies and evil minded. To such rivals the White man used his gun to quiet and suppress them. It is the same system of leadership that the Africans inherited upon independence. This particular approach has been condemned by the West when used by the African governments, but they forget they introduced it to Africa.

By making sure the African traditional system of government was changed, the Europeans set path for Africa's future crisis. It was a method of ensuring that Africa remained under their mercy and control, a thing that is true today. If Africa was left alone, it would have developed by itself. It may have taken long to do so but development would have been realized. Such development would have been detrimental to Europe that developed through Africa's reaping. It would mean Europe would not be as highly developed as it is today.

If all the wealth taken to Europe is brought back to Africa, the continent would experience great change. However, the Europeans would do anything possible to prove their genuine and non-guilt motives for Africa. They will blame Africans for the problems in the continent. But for those who understand the whole history, they know the truth. That Europeans are to blame for African under-development and current conditions. The truth hurts, and this certainly hurts the West. But it cannot be reversed, it is the whole truth.

The Africans exploitation by their colonial masters was not confined to Africa alone. Many Africans participated in major world wars between European powers. They fought and served as allies of their colonizers. Take the example of the French government war against Germans in Europe. In this war, over 180,000 West Africans served as French armies. They were also involved in another war against Germans in Togoland and the Cameroon. And on its part, the Germans at the beginning of the war had only 216 Europeans in Tanganyika and a total of 2,540 Africans. The British also used Africans in different wars, both in East Africa and West Africa. It should be noted that during these wars, the European proportion was kept minimal especially in Africa while the Africans were numerous. In many cases, the Africans fought one another as they supported their colonizers (rivals). This led to the death of many of them while only few European allies died. An African's life was worthless compared to that of an European. Even Europeans could shoot and kill Africans in order to instill fear and be obeyed by other Africans.

CHAPTER FIVE

NATURE IS TO BLAME FOR DEVELOPMENT CRISIS: FAMINE, DROUGHT AND FLOOD

Food queues, water rationing, and power cuts are all drought-caused hardships. Add to this the dramatically escalating prices for food, ... yet more trouble has cropped up in the form of strikes and go-slows (African Report, 1992:25).

INTRODUCTION

Drought in Africa has shattered the dreams of many Africans. The drought effect has replaced sweet memories with painful and sad memories. As once fertile and beautiful land turns to dust, crops and livestock die, then the core of an African is shaken. His future looks bleak and misty. Neither his mind nor his eyes "see" clearly, as life appears doomed. Drought invasion means there is no food, no water, no jobs, no strength to work, no motivation, and no life. And as such, more and more of his friends die. As he buries them, tears are easy to trickle down as he remembers he might be next or his child. The pain of drought is well expressed by an African farmer who noted; "you are better of dying from an automobile accident than from drought. An accident kills once. Drought kills like cancer".

DROUGHT AND DEVELOPMENT

The effects of drought and famine in Africa is said to contribute greatly to lack of effective development especially in the sub-Sahara region. For development to take place, there must be self-sufficiency in food, shelter and security. People must feel self-worth and dignity and have freedom to choose from increased material wealth and investments. In such an economy, there is joy and satisfaction. People have the ambition and self-motivation to work and produce, both now and in the future. But in Africa, drought is to blame for lagging development. With the coming of drought, food crops fail, cash crops fail, animals die, people die and vegetation disappears. This means the economy is paralyzed. No input for industries thereby lowering output. The people are not strong to work, have less purchasing power to buy the goods produced - which are expensive due to low supply while demand remains high. As prices escalate, majority of the people are left with no alternative but to die of hunger. It is at this juncture that donors and other organizations assist with food. Thousands upon thousands of Africans have died due to lack of food. To make the matter worse, after drought, heavy rains result. These often wash away all top soil, carry all seeds to lower lands or to the seas, and sometimes drown people. The life of an African is made even more miserable because his seeds are eroded by heavy rains and he has no money to buy more seeds. Unless he gets free seeds from the government or other agencies, his life and that of his family is in danger.

Analysts have seen drought as being a major hindrance to development in Africa especially in the region South of Sahara. It is not a drought that is there today and tomorrow is gone. It is a drought that continues. Some analysts feel that probably the type of crops grown in Africa especially imported seeds may not be suitable for the continental climatic change patterns. To show the seriousness of drought in Africa and its effect upon the people and the economy, in his article entitled "The Big Scorcher", appearing in *African Report,* (May - June, 1992), Andrew Medrum notes:

> The worst drought of the 20th century is burning up Southern Africa, exacerbating the plight of fragile economics. Hardest hit has been the region's staple food, maize, which has been devastated from coast to coast, requiring the import of 11 million tons of the crop and stretching severely strained

transport network. Some are now questioning the wisdom of
being so dependent on a non-drought resistant food (p.25).

The author further terms the drought as a natural disaster of biblical
proportions, this being the worst drought this century.

Africa seems to be on the wrong side of events. Natural disasters
and other misfortunes work together all at once. It is as if Africa has
wronged God and is cursed. While the drought takes its course of
ensuring that no crops survive on the face of the continent, civil wars,
economic upheaval, political mistrust and victimization are heavily
widespread. Country after country cries as a result of all the evils.
Refugees are on the move crossing one border to the next. It is a life
full of discouragement. Added to these problems the outside world is
on Africa exercising its power - forcing Africa to adopt Western
system of democracy. This has put Africa at a frustrated situation No
peace, no trust and no hope.

THE PUBLIC OUTCRY

The African people like any other people on earth, when crisis arise
turn to the governments. Much blame and condemnation are weighed
on the governments. Different groups would come together and oppose
any move or effort by the governments to either change the existing
situations or assist people. In their response to any opposition, African
governments are known to advocate a defensive approach.
Suppression of the opposition group is seen as a virtue and source of
strength for the governments. This often leads to civil war - between
the governments and the opposing groups, often called guerrilla
movements. The civil wars are numerous all over Africa. According
to Anne Shepherd in her article -- "Conflict", "... since 1960, 20 wars
have been fought on the African continent, killing 7 million people,
turnings 5 million into refugees, and wrecking millions of dollars in
destruction and havoc on struggling economies"(*Africa Report,* (May
- June 1992 p.40).

It is in this kind of life that an African finds himself. He is faced
with drought, and famine (natural), civil wars (African origin) and
democratization (outsiders' interference). In this situation, he is not
sure of what to do. To live or die; To develop or destroy; To escape or
stay. Whichever decision he takes, he has to live with it.

Most people would ask, but where did all there problems start from.

In a healthy economy, it is difficult to have hunger, insecurity and wars. People are busy struggling to build their economy that they have no time to think of evils about each other or their nations. Of course there may be few exceptions to this observation. Where the economy is bad, people are dissatisfied. In Africa, the economy of most countries is agricultural based. Drought means there is no agriculture or agricultural products produced. People are idle and have nothing to do. The Bible says that "an idle mind is the devil's workshop".

It is only when people are busy that we can expect progress. Drought in Africa has not led to progress but backwardness. It is the root of all the crisis as the argument goes. Let us explore this issue further is our discussion. Drought leads to lack of raw materials for industries thus low production. Low production means unemployment which in turn leads to low investments and savings. The result is increased poverty, a problem facing more than half of the African population.

THE LOCATION OF THE AFRICAN CONTINENT AND DROUGHT

Africa as a continent rests at the center of the earth. It is the only continent with three major tropical lines which determine the climatic conditions of the earth. To the north, the Tropic of Cancer, central is the Equator, and to the south is the Tropic of Capricorn. The regions to the North of the Tropic of Cancer and south of the Tropic of Capricorn are subject to cool and mild climate most of the year. The places are further from the Equator thus far from direct sun scorching. The region to the south of the Tropical of Cancer, north of Tropic of Capricorn and on the both side of the Equator have direct access to the sun. Africa's massive region is on this area. It is in this area that drought has taken its amazing but destructive trend. The region has about 20 of the world poorest states. Two to three years out of five are drought years. This means that four to six years out of ten are drought years. It has been difficult to predict when drought will come or end. In fact, it is possible to have much harvest this year and none in the next two years. Farmers are deceived by the unreliable weather which may appear very promising especially during planting season. As soon as the seeds have been planted, the rainy weather changes turning into a hot dry weather which kills all planted seeds. Soon there is no pasture for livestock or food for people and soon death starts "smelling" as it gets nearer. A reality no body likes apprehending.

Drought respects no boundaries or communities. As it burns south of the Sahara, it stretches from the Atlantic Ocean to the west of the Indian ocean. And as it stretches, it makes sure it leaves no plant surviving especially maize, the staple food for most people and chief source of income. Only drought resistant grains like millet and sorghum survive. Of late, the African governments have started to encourage farmers to plant more and more of their indigenous food crops. In the meantime, food imports continue to wreck the governments' financial stability. There are many examples in Africa of governments frustrated by drought which has left them almost financially handicapped. Money that is usually planned for other activities is diverted to pay for food imported to save people's life. For instance, after Namibia lost 80 per cent of its maize through drought, the government had to spend much foreign currency to import food. The money was originally meant to improve education and housing. Similarly, other countries have often adjusted their budgets to meet emergency in food crisis. Lesotho normally expects 120,000 tons of maize annually. But by 1992, she only expected 45,000 tons of maize. Likewise, Malawi produced only 700,00 tons as compared to its normal 1.4 million tons (*African Report,* May - June 1992:26).

Nearly every country South of the Sahara has to deal with this type of unexpected situation. The situation has frustrated governments and people alike. It is difficult to plan for the future. Sometimes the governments use different measures to rectify the situation. But often, such measures are not popular among the population and can lead to strong dissatisfaction. Take the example of the Zambian government. Its effort to try and remove the subsidy and increase the prices of maize (major staple grain in the country) in both 1986 and 1990 led to great protest in form of riots. The effect was so great that people started to advocate democracy as a mean of exercising justice. The consequence to the government was its defeat during the first democratic election polls in the country's history. The president by then, Dr. Kenneth Kaunda, could not convince his people that he could improve their living standard. His governments was a sign of oppression and people wanted liberty. However, the people's elected government has had its taste of the bitter pills of drought. Although it promised to make Zambians better economically, its economic structural adjustment program has suffered a great blow from drought.

But the Zambians seem to favor the present government in comparison to the previous government. At least it has not touched their source of life -- maize. It has not increased prices in away that would cause uproar. In the neighboring country, Zimbabwe faced a similar problem. While the people blamed the government for food shortage, the government was squeezed at a corner of political difficulties. As people queued for food, they still had to queue for water rationing. Industrial and domestic power had to be controlled and prices of domestic commodities continued to escalate on a daily basis, not to mention higher school fees and hospital charges.

The behavior of economic difficulties explained above is repeated in every country South of the Sahara apart from South Africa. Countries like Kenya, Tanzania, Malawi, Angola, Mozambique, Namibia, Uganda and Somalia have had their share of the drought impact.

DROUGHT IMPLICATION IN AFRICA

Drought in Africa has had some natural and historical implications. For instance, take Niger, a West African country. The country relies on the mighty Niger River for most of her domestic activities - agriculture. However, during the 1983-85 drought, the giant river did what the African tradition would consider a punishment to the society from the ancestors. A strong wind from the Sahara desert blew south ward making the river to 'dry' leaving only a string of stagnant pools and lagoons. It was the first time in living memory that this happened. This was a sure blow to Niger as a country where over three million people were directly affected. The effect was too great that some 400,000 nomads had migrated to the cities by June 1985. The nomads migrated to look for jobs and food since their source of life - River Niger- was no more. During this period, pastoralists lost up to 90 percent of their livestock. In his book, *The Greening of Africa: Breaking Through In The Battle For Land And Food: An International Institute For Environment And Development - Earthscan Study* (1987), Paul Harrison has noted that during the 1983-85 drought, almost eight million Ethiopian experienced drought. And in Sudan, during the same period, the lowest level of the Nile River flood was recorded in 350 years. This affected some ten million people. About 1.4 million refugees from neighboring Ethiopia and Chad who had fled from civil wars also suffered from severe drought. By 1985, the peak of the crisis, some 30 million Africans had felt the impact of drought. About 10 million of them had abandoned their homes in search of food. In all over Africa, North, South, East and West, a total of 24 countries had to deal with the epidemic (p. 17-18). The countries economic prosperity were made stagnant and some experienced negative growth. It is a situation which may take at least two decades to recover. In the meantime, the challenge still remains, how will Africa ever alter the consequence of drought and its spread in the continent? Even before the 1983-1985 drought, Africa had continued to experience a decline in food production at the rate of 12 percent during the period between 1965 and 1982. The decline was even severe in the mid 1980s and early 1990s. The consequence of food decline as a result of drought has been malnutrition and poverty increase. This has been de scribed as the most acute physical expression on absolute poverty. "It is poverty imprinted on human flesh and bone" (p.21).

ARE THE AFRICAN GOVERNMENTS TO BLAME FOR DROUGHT?

The problem of drought is not new to Africa as some may think. It is easy to blame African governments as responsible for mismanaging resources -- both human and natural. Forest clearing for cultivation purpose has reduced dense vegetation. This practice is said to lead to the possibility of lack of rain in many areas leading to drought. But a look at the history of the continent shows that it is difficulty to judge or conclude the real cause of drought. It may be natural climatic change in the universe or some other natural changes. Even as early as the beginning of this century, a decade long drought hit the continent. Notable was 1911-1914 drought that reduced the annual discharge of the Nile River by 35 percent while the depth of Lake Chad was reduced by half, not to mention the numerous other lakes and rivers that dried or had their levels reduced substantially. This problem was confined to the northern part of the continent, from Cape Verde to the horn of Africa.

There has been a noticeable change in climate in the second half of the twentieth century. It is during this second half that drought has intensified in Africa. It shows there could be some correlation between climatic change and current drought frequency in Africa.

Since the 1950s the average annual rainfall has declined in many parts of the continent. According to Kevin Shillington (1989:426), recent research points out that there is the possibility of a general world climatic change. The change is probably caused "by increasing pollution of the atmosphere in the industrial northern hemisphere". The pollution is associated with the increase incidence of drought in the Sahelian and Savannah zones of Africa. Unless devises are developed to control pollution in the northern hemisphere, then there is the possibility that drought in Africa will remain an enemy to the Africans. It is sad if the problems are man-made notably Europeans who condemn Africans as incapable of controlling the environmental crisis. The problem of drought may intensify in the future given the rate of industrialized in the northern hemisphere and in the African urban cities. It is unfortunate that African cities are the most unclean as compared to other parts of the world. This would make it difficult for the countries to device methods for controlling pollution.

Do we therefore conclude that drought as it applies to Africa is a now and future threat to development? That whether Africans like it or not they cannot solve the problem? This means we accept the poverty-stricken and absolute poverty level in Africa as a virtue that no man can change. This is probably the conclusion of most Africans who have suffered for decades. All they wait for is a miracle from God to transform their lives, not from governments. The Africans do not see any hope coming in their life time. Probably the future of their children may be bright, they just hope but never sure. After all, their parents hoped for bright a future for them. The truth is that, the children are due to have a more worse and severe life than their parents.

THE ROLE OF GOVERNMENT IN CONTROLLING DROUGHT

We cannot take the current discussion as useless. It is important to analyze the level of development in Africa and the consequences of drought. Because the governments know very well that no five years can go without a drought taking place in their countries, why not plan and have enough food and other products for use during the poor economic period. Why can't governments spend money on building better storage facilities to keep all harvests - during period of booms. They can use such harvest during time of drought and their people will not suffer. The food can then be distributed to the needy population. Likewise, the governments can train their farmers,(majority of Africans) on better methods of cultivation, research on resistance crops to replace maize which is not a drought crop although it gives high yield. The governments know their population growth and output expected to meet the demand. Through effective planning and prediction, the fateful effects of drought upon the population can be reduced to a manageable level.

It shows that drought although present in Africa, it may not be solely blamed for all crisis in the continent. Governments in Africa need to be blamed for drought's effects where it involves deaths of their populations. Instead of preparing through good planning, governments seem not to care about their people. It is easy for the governments to plan and invest on prestigious projects and expensive dams and irrigation schemes which later fail due to poor management, lack of spare parts or being misplaced in the wrong locations and thus become unproductive. Added to this is the governments' efforts of spending billions upon billions on military arms for protecting against any opposition from the poor hungry people. The people may be trying to register their hunger and suffering with the governments, but instead of listening, the governments suppress and attack the people. Angry and disappointed, the people take arms to fight the governments. After all, what is the use of a government which cannot serve or listen to the people? The effect is civil war, a frequent uprising in Africa. Many examples of governments fighting their hungry people can be found in many countries in Africa when the governments don't want to admit their failure. Take the case of Chad, Sudan and Ethiopia - during the 1970s and 1980s drought, the countries experienced civil wars - yet many people were hunger stricken. In Ethiopia, the government which took power in 1974 after overthrowing Haile Selassie spent half of the country's annual revenue upon arms to fight rebels in Tigre and Eritrea during the 1980s. The two areas had experienced great famine. What a tragedy? The same story has been repeated in Mozambique and Angola. It is sad that during drought leading to famine, when majority of people are suffering, civil wars are frequent against the hungry communities. The governments would spend on arms rather than on food.

It is ironical that during boom periods when food is plenty, a lot of it rots in the farms due to lack to good infrastructure. Poor roads, lack of bridges make it difficult for farmers to reach markets. And whatever get to the market is usually bought at low prices. Demand is less compared to supply. For staple food like maize and wheat which can be stored for future use, the governments may export the commodities to make quick money. But the same food exported will be imported during drought and at a higher price. This indicates how the governments facilitate droughts' effect rather than control it.

CONCLUSION

The current discussion has focused on drought and other natural disasters facing Africa. Although drought has had a long and severe consequences on the African continent, the discussion points out that drought is not solely to blame for African crisis. This natural epidemic has existed in Africa since time immemorial. However, man has interfered with the ecological system thus prolonging the drought and making it more frequent than in the past. Industrialization in the northern atmosphere has caused pollution which has interfered with the natural pat tern of the climatic change. Pollution has increased and spread southward. Likewise, pollution from industries in Africa and the increasing late of dumping has worsened the situation. Again the blame like in the past chapter is on man -- Europeans and Africans.

The African governments bears the biggest burden of blame for drought - famine effect. There are numerous ways of controlling the effect of drought especially food shortage, high prices, riots and deaths resulting from hunger. The governments have failed to plan and develop better storage facilities to cater for dry periods. Rather than storing food and other products, the governments have sold the products to outsiders - export - during booms only to import the same products at high prices when their people start starving. This does not sound logical although the governments claim they need foreign currency and are to pay for increasing debts.

The drought - famine - flood's effects have been worsened by civil wars facing the same countries. Instead of looking for everlasting solutions to the crisis that may be present, the governments have suppressed the opposing groups without exploring the reason for complaining. Most of those suppressed are termed as traitors and agitators. Where the suppression fails, the governments are sometimes overthrown and replaced other governments which may promise survival for the suffering. Words are easier said than deeds. Soon the new governments become victimizers of oppression rather than saviors. And the vicious-cycle is repeated. Drought comes again, people die, governments fail, economies collapse, poverty widen and the future become dark, no hope. Then all people and governments blame drought as the cause of the under-development in Africa. And this becomes the "core" cause of poverty. Probably because drought is nature related and it cannot defend itself. Man can defend himself if blamed. But evading the truth does not solve the problems of Africa. They only worsen. It is treating the symptoms, not the real diseases.

CHAPTER SIX

SLAVE TRADE AND UNDER -DEVELOPMENT

Masters, provide your slaves with what is right and fair, because you know that you also have a master in heaven (Colossians 4:1 - NIV).

INTRODUCTION

The issue of slave trade and its effect to African development has been treated with mixed feelings. Some people have not seen anything evil with the practice while others see the practice as evil and inhuman. For several centuries, Africans were traded as slaves, both by the Arabs and the Europeans. But it was the Europeans that made sure that the trade was profitable and prosperous. To many historians, slave trade was complex and more deeply rooted than many people think. It was a practice that is said to have wrecked Africa's capability of development and political structural adjustment. The social, political and economical systems of the Africans were deeply affected. In some cases, some communities were shattered and wiped from the face of the earth.

BACKGROUND TO SLAVE TRADE

Before exploring the effects of this evil business, it is wise to first understand the background of the practice, from an African point of view as well as from an outsider (Europeans especially).

Since the year 700 AD, some eight hundred years ago, Africans contact with the outside world was with the Muslims, Arabs.

The contact was mainly by land across the Sahara Desert or by sea along the Eastern Coast of Africa. However, upon contact with the Europeans in the 15th century, the communication with the outside world changed its patterns. Instead of using both land and sea as previously done, sea became the dominant source of access to outside world. Likewise, the Muslims' contact was minimal as Europeans influence increased from both Western Africa and Eastern African coasts. The trans-Saharan trade which had existed for centuries was replaced by ships from European countries that patrolled the seas and traded for gold, ivory and slaves. The Europeans' arrival marked a new history for Africa, a history that was to continue for over four centuries.

Slavery in Africa like in any other continent was not new. Like in the Middle East, slavery in Africa had been practiced since ancient times. It was slavery that involved the poor who needed food, war victims and voluntary slaves. It was not harsh and was accepted by different communities. Commercial state trade was first organized by the Arabs mostly along the Eastern coast of Africa. It was the Arabs who first used slaves from Africa and exported them across the Indian Ocean to East Indies. When the Europeans took over the trade in the 15th Century, some thirty million slaves were shipped to America from West Africa. This figure can be doubled considering the fact that for every slave sold to a colonial master or plantation owner, another lost his life on the way due to the cruel round-up at home or in the crowded health hazard slave ships. It shows how Africa lost most of its people in the most crudest form of dealing with human beings.

Slave trade in Africa has been termed as the greatest crime in history. Both Europeans and Africans have been condemned for accepting and promoting the evil practice. Africans were hunted like rats and chained together before being sold. It is unfortunately that, African leaders in some communities encouraged and benefited from the trade's profit. They captured slaves from the African hinterland and then delivered them to European traders along the coast. Some states and kingdoms boosted their economies and power from the trade. They raided small communities and sold them for money or in exchange of other European products. Notable traders in West Africa were states like Benin, Oyo, Ashanta, and Dahomey.

EFFECTS OF SLAVERY

The results of slave trades in the West African region were numerous. For instance, slave raiding promoted inter-tribal wars, the depopulation of raided areas, and indifferences among Africans themselves. European authors have argued that slave trade led to new contact between the Africans and the Whites, a contact that is termed beneficial. They are attributed to the introduction of new life. Style based on new medicines, tools, new crops - cassava, maize and sweet potatoes. This increased food supply. Slave raids were also said to have checked population increase in the regions affected. The conclusion and observation fail to address the most important evil resulted from the practice - abuse of human life and dignity. It introduced the opinion of viewing some people as inferior (slaves) and others as superior (African raiders). It was the start of ethnic differences in Africa. By the time slave trade was finally abolished, the Europeans and American masters had gotten great wealth from the trade. This explains why there was laxity in the final abolition of the practice. For instance, English Parliament abolished slavery in 1833, France in 1848, Netherlands in 1863, and Portugal in 1878. The United States was greatly affected by civil war which made it impossible to continue the practice. From laxity, it is clear that slave trade although considered evil by anti-slavery groups, it was more valued in terms of its economic gains, rather than human dignity. It is sad that no African leader was ready to fight for his people to be freed. The major interest of leaders was states' wealth. This encouraged the European traders who influenced their governments towards trade justification. Even after slave trade was officially abolished, most European countries continued with the illegal habit. Slaves were captured and shipped to East Indies, Central America and Southern United States. However, those who fought for freedom did not give up. In the United States, for example, both Blacks and Whites abolitionists organized a secret Underground Railroad to help slaves escape to free states or across the border to Canada (WallBank et al. 1960: 176 Vol 2).

WHY AFRICANS BECAME VICTIMS OF SLAVERY?

But why were African slaves preferred in relation to other people? The development of large plantations, gold and silver mines meant that a large imported labor force was required. This was especially the case in the Americans and the Caribbean's. The local population in these areas were not well suited for the labor force. The local indigenous population, for example, quickly succumbed to the harsh treatment of the European colonizers and were seriously affected by unfamiliar European diseases, for instance, smallpox. One century after their contact with the Europeans, ninety percent or more of the Caribbean islands people had died. This was attributed to harsh and violence treatments or diseases. To solve the problem, European colonizers transported criminals and outcasts to America from Europe notably in the 16th century. But the demand was more than supply. To make matters worse, those sent died from tropical diseases. This was a blow to the colonizers who could not rely on the local or those from Europe. It was in this desperate state that the colonizers turned to Africa.

There was some logic in turning to Africans as a source of labor. The Africans had a certain level of immunity to some tropical diseases which other races could not survive. Also, the Europeans wanted to take the advantage of the African skills and experience in metal-working, mining and tropical agriculture, a known art.

Having being in the African coast, the Portuguese for example, had used Africans as labor force in their sugar plantations in the rich volcanic soil of the equatorial islands of Principe and Sao Tome. From their contact with the Africans, the Portuguese had learnt that there were some African leaders along the coast who were prepared to sell their war captives and criminals. The Africans were also considered to be better and strong workers.

STARTING OF COMMERCIAL SLAVERY IN AFRICA

The first African slaves from West African coast were transported across the Atlantic and sold in 1532. This started the trans-Atlantic trade in human cargo, a distance of some 6,500 kilometers. At first the number of slaves was small. But after 1630s when different European states got involved in sugar plantations in Brazil and the Caribbean's, the demand for slaves increased.   Notable countries were the Dutch, the French, and the English people. The increased trade marked the largest scale force transportation of human captives in history.

The annual increase in slaves from Africa was gentle and reached its pick in the eighteenth century. Although historians have not concluded as to the actual number of slaves transported annually, a rough estimation has shown that at least ten millions Africans landed alive and sold in America and the Caribbean. Annual number shows that an average of 20,000 slaves were transported in the 17th century, and between 50,000 and 100,000 a year during the 18th century. Considering the number of those who died on the way, it is probable that we may never agree on the correct figure.

SHOULD WE BLAME AFRICANS OR EUROPEANS FOR SLAVE TRADE?

On the whole, the Europeans took slaves with the goal of using them to increase their wealth. They promoted the trade as beneficial and cheap to manage. Much blame on this trade may rest on the Europeans for trading human beings and using them as material   possessions. However, major blames rest on the Africans. In fact, the European traders were not active in capturing slave victims. This was done by Africans. The European traders did not go into the interior for raids. This would have been very expensive and risky. In any case, they suffered great losses whenever they tried to penetrate in to the inland. They also died of tropical diseases. It was the Africans who did the raid expeditions and brought the victims to the coast for sale. While some Africans were specialists in the trade, some African chiefs and kings received tributes for assisting the traders.

Although some slaves were war captives removed from the society for good, most captives sold were the product of wars waged for the purpose. And as the price offered rose, the number of wars also increased. The more slaves sold, the richer the African middlemen became. This was a big motivation to raid more slaves.

WHO GAINED FROM SLAVERY? - EFFECTS AND IMPACT

The ethnic differences were central to the slave trade business. While some ethnic groups became very rich as a result of the practice, others were humiliated and weakened completely. Some were wiped completely from existence. It is worth noting that the African rulers who sold war captives, rarely sold people from their own ethnic groups unless they were unwanted by the society - criminals and outcasts. The big states also took the advantage of raid to expand their local lands and power. This was particularly so when war was waged against small stateless societies.

Economically, the strong states became rich and powerful. the weak became weaker and poorer. But there was even a bigger problem. Those sold could not play their role of developing Africa as they lost contact with Africa. If they were not sold, I believe they would have helped in the development and promotion of agriculture and other skillful activities, unique to Africa.

Secondly, those sold were the young and most productive section of the society. Their ages ranged between 14 years and 35 years, a young and youthful age. It meant the group was to go and contribute to the growth and development of America and Europe, outside economies. This was a major mistakes on the part of the Africans which was done due to greed for power and wealth.

Thirdly, was the depopulation and distortion of the development of the African continent. While some states or regions were completely depopulation, some became centers of high population density. This led to imbalanced development in Africa. It was those areas in touch with Europeans that were developed while others remained remote and under-developed.

The greatest evil as explained earlier was that of disregarding human life as useless. Once captured, a slave ceased to be a human being. He became a property. There was no difference between a slave and a donkey, a goat, an ax, or a hoe. He belonged to the master who could do what he wanted. Also he could be sold again or be killed without a question.

SLAVE TRADE: HOW INHUMAN?

The inhuman element was demonstrated from the time a slave was captured to the time of death. According to Kevin Shillington in his book, *History of Africa* (1989):

> Captives were chained together and marched to the coast where they were chained together in rows and forced to lie on specially constructed trading ship. They were then stripped naked, men and women together, and examined minutely to see if they were fit, strong and healthy. Once a deal had been struck between African middleman and European slave merchant the most terrible part of their voyage began. On board ship they were chained together in rows and forced to lie on specially constructed 'decks' which were arranged like shelves barely half a meter one above the other .... They lay like this for weeks on end, suffering in the stench of their own excrete and urine and given barely enough food and water to keep them alive. Those that died were simply thrown overboard. On average between fifteen and thirty percent could be expected to die from disease, maltreatment or exhaustion during the three to six weeks of the trans-Atlantic crossing. .... In this manner tens of thousands of Africa's fittest young men and women were removed from the continent every year, all in the name of profit for European merchants and plantation owners (1989:176-177).

It is sad to note that neither European merchants nor plantation owners saw any evil in the practice. To the ship merchants, this was a business like any other business -- profit was the goal. From Europe to Africa, ship brought European goods; from Africa to America, slaves were traded; and finally sugar from America to Europe. All this led to high profits. Once across the Atlantic, slaves were sold for two or three times their cost in the African coast. In other cases, they could be exchanged for sugar which was to be sold in Europe.

It was this profit motive that most analysts have condemned. The profit drive made the European merchants, plantation owners, and manufacturers to disregard any human worthiness of an African. They did not care for the continent where they removed the Africans. An African could not be expected to develop Africa from his brutal and savagery state. He was first to be rescued from that state. Slavery was viewed as a form of liberating him, not undermining development.

The above reason is illogical and self-centered as the motive of getting slaves from Africa. The Europeans cheated African rulers to raid their people and enslave them. If the Africans needed to be civilized, why didn't they start with those African leaders they used as middlemen? Why go to the weak? And if they wanted to rescue an African, why didn't they free them when they got to America or Caribbean? This was another excuse to oppress the Africans but which needed to be condemned before it started. It was after Europe had started to develop other methods of production -- industrial revolution, that slaves were released. Their benefits were no more and so abolition became possible.

SLAVE TRADE AND UNDER-DEVELOPMENT

Compared to other continents where outside contacts led to great prosperity - export of local made products or cash crops, African contact with the West led to a situation were its people was the main export, not for development but for destruction purpose. Assessment of the kind of destruction resulting from slave trade is hard to realize, in fact probably the best measure of what actually happened is by measuring how Africa's creative energy would have developed the continent if the human trade did not take place. With unity of different ethnic groups, Africa would surely be a success in one way or another.

It is notable to see that Europeans' involvement in slave trade was pioneered by the Portuguese. Having discovered that Africans were good source of unpaid labor, they spread their practice to other colonies. Before other powers got involved in the trade, it is estimated that the Portuguese had exported over a quarter of a million slaves. Although British later on took the lead in the abolition of slavery, it was after she had reaped great profit from the trade. During the 18th century, Britain was the principle maritime power. As such, half of all the slaves along the Trans-Atlantic route were transported in British ship. Britain got a lot of profit as it monopolized the market. Slaves exported from West Africa were enormous. It is hard to estimate their number but analysts believe that about 20 millions may have been exported between Senegal and Angola hinterland.

Effort to free and stop the evil trade was often ignored by Western European powers who saw the trade as an economic necessity. A country feared to leave the trade in fear that others will continue. But efforts to free slaves had continued as far back as 1772 when about 15,000 slaves were freed after England recognized the trade as illegal. Similarly, in 1820 some free Negroes were settled by the American Colonization Society at Monrovia, present day capital of Liberia. The slaves freed had some difficulties adjusting in Africa. Having no tribal roots, they only spoke English and were greatly influenced by the European ways of life under the care of the Christian missionaries. The groups both in Freetown and Monrovia were no different from Americans or British. It was also difficult and hard for them to penetrate to the interior because people in the interior could not understand or accept them. This explains why they settled along the coast and remained as different cultural communities compared to the local inhabitants who were rooted in traditional customs and beliefs.

Although the true figure of all slaves exported to America is hard to know, in 1969 a statistical assessment by Professor Philip Curtis stated that a total of over eleven million slaves were transported from Africa to America. He observed that about 80 percent of the total took place in the period 1701 - 1850. Breaking the figure on century basis, he stated that before 1600 AD, 330,000 slaves were exported; 1601 - 1700, 1,609,000; 1701-1810, 7,262,000; and 1811-1870, 2,278,000 (in Roland Olive et. al. 1981:145). Of particular regions, Senegambia alone exported about one third of the total slaves that left Africa prior to   1600.   Another area that continued to produce slaves was Juta Jalon region.   Areas like that between Sierra Leone and the Gold Coast were not greatly affected by slavery due to the absence of natural harbors, and treacherous offshore conditions which made it difficult for European shipping. States like Oyo, Ashanti and Dahomey were rivals to other tribes. They raided them, ceased them and enslaved them for sale. They then expanded their state regions and took more land especially gold mines which made them even more wealthier. Along the Eastern Africa, towns like Kilwa, Mombasa, and Zanzibar islands were key trading centers.

Conclusion

Slave trade in Africa and outside has much to do with the European attitude toward the Africans. Because they did not respect an African, their concern was minimal. In fact, it was the Europeans who introduced the money system in Africa and convinced the Africans to use it to sell their brothers and sisters. If it were possible to reverse the trend, then the Europeans would have become slaves for just one year. It would be a good experience to demonstrate how slave trade was to be conducted and how Africans felt.

Thanks to all those who fought the evil practice. It shows that not all Europeans and Africans are the same. While some are evil, others are value human life. They have love and concern for fellow human beings, whether White or Blacks. These are the people that we need in the society, any society. Christian missionaries like Dr. David Livingstone and William Wilberforce are to be recognized for their efforts to fight the deadly practice. They knew Africans needed more than selfish and unbalanced trade. Africans required development not hatred between ethnic groups. The European traders knew that without this hatred, no trade would take place. But Christians knew that harmony among the tribes was vital for all human races. Material and wealth accumulation could only promote differences between the haves and have not. This is a practice which has existed since and continue to plague Africa. No matter how anyone may look at the issue of slave trade in Africa or outside, the fact is that the practice was a demonstration of little value for human dignity. It did not only lead to under-development of Africa, it also divided the Africans on the basis of the strong and the weak societies, not to mention those people left and abandoned and in the New World. With no cultural ties to Africa, no common language, the slaves' identity was lost. As many wonder all over the world as free citizens of other continents, the question still remains for them. What did we do to deserve all these? To be foreigners, exiles, hated, mistreated and abused. Yet, they have no place they can call home. Like the Jewish who longed to go back to Israel, the land of their forefathers, the Africans taken as slaves have the same urge. To come to Africa, at least once in their life-time. But the question is: will the African governments give them a chance? It may be the beginning of a new relationship and change in Africa.

CHAPTER SEVEN

MULTINATIONALS: THE NEW COLONIZERS IN AFRICA

What have these big companies done for the country? Nothing. The concessions were given with the hope that the companies would develop the country. They have exploited it, which is not the same thing as development; they have bled and squeezed it like an orange whose skin is sooner or later discarded (Adre Gide).

INTRODUCTION

The issue of multinationals and their role in development of a country have been questioned. Multinational corporations have especially been strong in the last two decades that it has even become difficult to control their activities. As compared to the past when these big companies were confined in their home countries, today most of them see their market as global rather than domestic. With huge capital to venture into new areas, the corporations have explored any possibility of global expansion that may provide feasible source of raw materials or new markets. Most of the companies have great sales as compared to host countries gross national products (GNP) or budgets.

Multinationals   activities in developing countries are notable because of their   great influence. They dictate prices, economical behavior, political stability and the living standard of the population. With big budgets and sources of capital compared to their hosts, they can afford to enforce decisions or policies to the host nations or states.

It is amazing how multinational corporations have increased over the years. They have not only increased in numbers but also in sizes. By 1975, more than 10,000 multinational corporations controlled over 50,000 affiliates outside their parent countries. The affiliates represented a book value of more than $165 billion. As may be expected, majority of the multinational corporations stem from developed countries where they flourish to other countries, especially developing countries - Africa, Southern Asia and Latin America. In fact about 80 percent of these corporations, foreign affiliates, and their international branches are from   five countries: United Kingdom, Germany, Switzerland, and United   States. However, when one include Japan and Canada, then the   involvement of multinational corporations would account for   almost 90 percent of international business (Sauvand and Lavipour, 1975:ix). And because their wealth is well distributed in different countries where they operate from, they are not dependent on a single country. This explains why they can pull out from one country without feeling major effects. Most of them are still owned and managed by their countries of origin.

As noted, the growth and expansion of multinational corporations has been tremendous in recent years. This change is well demonstrated by the growth in sales and book value of the origin   countries. For example, "the book value of total U.S. foreign   direct investment increased from $12 billion in 1950 to $33   billion in 1960 and exceeded $100 billion in 1974" (p.x). The increase also included the sizes of the multinationals and their numbers. For instance, between 1950 and 1966, the number of U.S. affiliates increased from 7,000 to 23,000, more than three time rise. Similarily:

> . . . the growth of investment flow has been reflected in the increase in its cumulative stock. Between 1960 and 1971, the book value of U.S. direct investment increased from $33 billion to $86 billion and that of the United Kingdom from $12 to $24 billion. The most dramatic increase, from less than $300 million to   approximately $4.5 billion, was registered by Japan - a fifteen fold rise. Recent indications show that this pace has continued if not accelerated. Almost equally impressive was the performance of the Federal Republic of Germany, which exhibited an almost tenfold increase of investment stock to $7.3 billion by 1971 (p.10)

During the period from 1950 to 1970, the United States gained greatly from multinational activities. At this period, the country's book value based on direct foreign investments skyrocketed from $11.8 billion to $78.1 billion. However, the dominance of Japan in the field was noticeable after 1970. In 1989, twenty of the top fifty firms in the world based on market value were Japanese. According to *Business Week*, July 16, 1990, these firms were primarily those in the sectors of electronics, oil, banking and telecommunications. Even among the top ten firms, only three were from United States. The IBM, a United States based, ranked second with market value of $68.89 billion. The top international firm in the world was Nippon Telegraph and Telephone which had a market value of $118.79 billion. This was almost twice the size of IBM, its closest rival. The Japanese dominance is expected to continue in 1990s. In its 1990 identification of the top twenty-five large public companies outside the United States, *Forbes* magazine, July 23, 1990, ranked Japanese firms as holding the top seventeen positions with European companies taking the other eight slots. Sumitomo Corporation topped the list with a revenue of $158.221 billion (in Khambata and Ajami, 1992:6-8). This conclusion shows the Japanese continued trend in expanding in the world of multinationals. It is an expansion which has worried both the Europeans and the Americans.

MULTINATIONALS DEFINED

But what are multinationals? It would be wrong to continue with a discussion of multinational corporations without first defining this system of business enterprise. Different scholars and business practitioners will define multinationals differently. According to some, multinationals are the businesses which conduct business in various countries but using one country as their headquarters. Others see multinationals as those businesses that have ownership held across a number of countries or where the product divisions are held at a global level. Similarly, the ratios of foreign ownership especially on assets or operations have been used to define multinationals. As such, firm classified as multinationals have their revenues, sales, shares, as sets, and personnel coming or located in diverse countries or regions. The behavior and attitude of the management can also be used to determine multinationals. While the management of multinationals may be centralized, most are decentralized. Thus, instead of carrying all management activities from one place or country, management is distributed in different countries. The countries are given the freedom to make decisions and implement them. In such cases, however, a board of directors is used to explore the effectiveness of the decisions and their viability. In many cases, multinationals still carry their behavior and attitudes as established in their headquarters or as per their country of origins expectations. As seen earlier, multinationals originate and are managed in developed countries although their activities, at least, 80 percent, are carried in developing countries.

One may wonder what leads to several definitions. It is worth understanding that all multinationals have different objectives and missions. This makes their operations different, thus their characteristics and definitions. Each one of them is unique and it is impossible to use one definition to fit all of them. The evolution of multinationals from domestic to international levels makes it difficult to label a company as multinational. Should we call a company a multinational while at its home? Probably that is why the United Nations restrains from the use of the term multinational. Instead, it uses the term transnational corporations. But to clear the confusion, I would use Dara Khambata and Riad Ajami conclusion on multinationals. The two scholars say they would use terms like multinationals corporations and multinational enterprises interchangeably "to identify a firm that conducts international business from a multitude of locations in different countries" (1992:6). It is a firm though has one country of origin, it has expanded beyond its country of origin's borders thereby making it an international firm in its operations. A simple definition would be to define a multinational company as a company involved in producing and marketing its products or services in several countries.

THE MULTINATIONALS AND COLONIAL GOVERNMENTS' CONNECTION

A comparison of multinationals and colonial governments shows some close relations. The colonial powers decided to acquire colonies when they needed more resources for their industries. And because their countries could not meet demand, then it was reasonable to go out (internationally) to get resources. Likewise, multinational corporations expand beyond their borders when their home markets are small compared to production. They thus go out to look for more markets. The markets are in either developed or developing countries.

It is in developing countries that multinationals are said to boost their profits. This results from low cost of production due to low labor costs, cheap and available raw material, and political freedom. They monopolize markets by restricting or destroying small in the industry. With dominant market, the firms charge higher prices to get supernormal profits. This is an expoitive means of doing business.

MULTINATIONALS IN AFRICA

In Africa, the role of multinationals is evident. They are everywhere strong and bearing much power. They frighten local industries by using their money to launch campaigns meant to fight the industries. They sometimes lower their prices for a period knowing that the local industries cannot afford to operate below production costs.

Of course, one may ask why are the African governments like other in developing countries unable to control multinational operations? There are several reasons:

1. They have plenty of money which is used to bribe government officials in some countries. This makes them continue operating.

2. With financial capability, they employ a majority of population. And because the governments have no jobs for the unemployed or those working for multinationals, they keep quiet. Opposing multinationals could lead to withdrawal from the host countries. This can lead to riots and strikes from those previously employed, and with poor living standards.

3. Most of these multinationals still carry the colonial power's authority. Most governments in Africa still rely on aid and other financial assistance from former colonial powers. Any move to oppose multinationals can be seen as opposing the colonial governments. This can be interpreted as a revolt against former colonial masters. It means the victim country is subject to financial aid or grant withdrawal and other supports.

4. With huge financial capability, multinationals have the ability to oust a government through direct or indirect involvement in the political affairs of a country. This way, a multinational can put a government of its favor in power. This threatening move makes many African governments quiet and humble even when they interpret a multinational's activities as undesirable.

The above activities show the presence of multinationals as being the presence of former colonial powers. In fact, multinationals are even worse than the colonial powers who were forced out of Africa. Multinationals are licensed in the host countries and are difficulty to remove. They have changed people's culture through their products, services, behaviors and attitudes. They have transformed the society from being domestic dependence to foreign-import dependence.

MULTINATIONALS: THE NEW COLONIZERS

With the coming of independence in Africa, many Africans thought this was the end of colonial influence in the continent. But they were wrong. Although the countries got their political independence, their resources continued to be exploited by the former colonies, this time, through Western companies. As a result, Africa became more and more dependence on the west. It provided cheap raw materials for European countries and North American industries. This is a situation which the African countries have not been able to come out while the companies continue to become stronger and stronger.

The African governments instead of making it difficult for the exploiting companies to come to Africa and establish themselves, the governments have willingly granted concessions to the companies. As a result, most of the mining and import-export businesses fall under multinationals.

One may expect the companies to have left the continent as former colonizers did. However, the opposite is true. Many continued to invade Africa before and after independence. They had to remain and continue pursuing the colonizers' interests as previously noted, enriching the West. Few examples show how the companies "seemed" not to be aware they were supposed to leave Africa upon independence. In Nigeria, during the eve of independence, the United Africa Company and the other subsidiaries were still controlling about half of the country's import trade business. And for many years, Firestone had taken advantage of cheap labor in Liberia thus its enormous profits. And when Liberia adopted American dollar as its currency in 1943, numerous companies came in great number. The greatest investment in Africa among multinationals started after the Second World War. Most countries having suffered economically turned to Africa as a source of raw cheap material and labor. United States for instance greatly invested in Africa after 1945. This is demonstrated by change of policy in 1947. The "so-called U.S. 'and ' to Europe under the 1947 Marshall Aid plan went to firms like the mines de Zellidja, which mined North Africa lead and zinc" (Mazrui and Tidy 1989:33). The Belgians on the other hand received economic aid from America to enable the government implement 'a ten-year economic programme in the Congo between 1950 and 1959" (p.33).

The point of cheap labor is mentioned elsewhere. But this seemed to be the key drive that brought and still brings foreign companies to Africa. The amount paid to an African worker is too little compared to elsewhere in the world. A United States miner, for example, earns an average 30 times than his counter part African working in mines in South Africa. It is this opportunity to exploit cheap labor in Africa that encourages White immigrants and businessmen from Europe after 1945 and during the 1960s. The target profits came from mines, urban trades and farming - plantations.

The number of traders and immigrants who came to do business thereby expanding multinationals activities from Europe or America was astonishing especially in Southern African region where diamond and gold were a big motivation for outsiders coming to the area. Between 1945 and 1960, South Africa alone gained a net of 87,772 immigrants, and 254,616 between 1961 and 1970. And in Zimbabwe, an annual figure of 16,000 Whites arrived during the post war period. On her part, Zambia (former Northern Rhodesia) received between 22,000 Whites in 1946 and by 1958, about 72,000 Whites were in the country. The immense number of Whites in the region meant increased activities of international businesses. The immigrants became agents of their own governments and home companies. They sent huge profits from Africa to their countries. By independence, African governments could not afford to root out the companies. Although few companies may have left Africa for fear of loosing their businesses, most remained to promote and create awareness about European products among Africans. This has led to a cultural change where the Africans now solely depend on Western imported products and services. The change has favored the multinationals who now have discovered new markets in Africa. And to make sure the markets are maintained, they have fought local businesses through price reduction and media campaigns. How superior and safe the products and services from the companies are, is another controversial matter. Yet most governments in Africa are handicapped. They have no power or financial capability of promoting local businessmen and industries to compete with these giants companies. This has made the companies to take control of the economies in Africa. They decide the climate and standard of living for majority who depend on their products. And because their goal is profit they care less about the safety, hygiene and the side effects of their products and services.

The major developed countries have substantial share of stock in developing countries. The more developed the countries are, the more involved in multinational operations in developing countries. The United States multinationals, for example, represent half of the total stock of foreign direct investment and activities in developing countries. There are countries where the U.S. accounts for almost two-thirds of the total stocks of foreign direct investment. Such countries are in Central and Latin America. In Africa on the other hand, the U.S. activities and direct investment have remained minimal with only one-fifth of the total stock. Britain on the other hand accounts 30 percent of direct foreign investment; France 26 percent; Belgium 7 per cent; Netherlands and Italy account for 5 and 4 percent respectively (Sauvand and Lavipour 1976:21-22). This involvement shows how Africa like the rest of the world has contributed toward America and Europe's wealth. The countries of Africa offer market for European and American corporations. While huge ex ports from these powers come to Africa, Africa itself exports very little because the bulk of produce comes from agriculture and service industries as compared to industrial goods imported to Africa.

The goal of companies started by colonial powers were to exploit the colonies to supply the mother countries with required raw materials. The materials were then converted into goods manufactured for export or substituted for imports mostly to the colonies. Such companies were granted charters to establish trading and production monopolies. To make sure the monopolies took effect, the companies activities were centralized. Attempts by other companies (local) to diversified trade were minimally encouraged by discriminatory tariffs. The practice made the colonial companies to grow tremendously. Some of the key-known multinationals were the British East India Company, the Dutch East India Company, and the Hudson's Bay Company.

To show the companies operations and power, P. T. Ellsworth notes:

The merchants of (the British East India Company)
received the entire rights over all of India that they could
bring under their way .... As its director, Sir Josiah
Child, once boasted, the India Company was 'a sovereign
state in itself'. It declared war on the Mogul Empire, it
had a fleet, an army, and fortified settlements, it could
coin money and make laws. Businessmen administered
India in their own fashion, and a very lively fashion it was
for a long time (1964:33).

Although the quoted behavior may not be present today among
multinationals operating in Africa, it is true that they still have a
monopoly of power to conduct business as they wish. Administered
from their home countries, their policies often do not reflect the host
country's desire. A commercial aired in the U.S. is easily used in
Africa without any adjustment. No cultural or social considerations
may be taken into account. As a result the Western culture is exported
to Africa. After all, the African should honor the provision of the
"superior" products or services provided by these giants.

HOW DANGEROUS ARE MULTINATIONALS?

The growth of the multinationals abroad has intensified. Africa like
many other third world regions has had its share. In its 1984 report,
the International Labor Organization in Geneva factually identified
over 2,000 third world multinationals. The actual figure was estimated
to be between 6,000 and 8,000 corporations. The argument being that
most of the LCD's now host and headquarters the corporations, a
more interpreted to mean that the host countries are now participating
in the multinational process (Kolde 1985:290-291). This observation
can be said to vary from one multinational to the next. Although they
offer employment to LCD's members and may adjust their activities to
fit the cultural and economic needs, most impose their culture and
behavior to the host countries. They may be headquartered in countries other than their homes, but as long as they don't change their
exploitive attitude and approach, they remain enemies to development
of Africa. If they operate independently and in corporation with host
government; if they share part of their profits with the governments
and society; if they localize their activities and management; and if
they change fair prices, then they can be considered worth and
concerned with the welfare of the people served. The LCD's
especially in Africa can identify with them. But as long as they

continue to charge high   prices; pay low wages; siphon profits to mother countries;   threatened the political structure of the host countries, then their role in development will remain minimal. They will continue to be seen as agents of post colonial masters even though some may not have any direct connections or similarities with such past powers. It is only through genuine motives and objectives that the corporations can be seen as sincere. If only they can value life; if only they can contribute toward development in a positive way, if only they can advice governments on the best trend to development; if only they are not selfish; and if only they love Africa, then they would care. They would not exploit and would improve the welfare and standard of living of the people. This is a noble call which they can try. It is possible.

In the meantime, as long as they still carry their present operations through undermining African resources, just like former   colonizers did, then the label "new colonizers" will continue to be applied to them. The multinationals have to prove that they are not colonizers, a challenge that is yet to be faced and realized.

To the Africans, a colonizer and multinational corporation may not have any difference. After all they are organized, managed, directed, controlled and monitored from abroad.   Where were the colonies organized and monitored? Abroad. Also, the colonizers occupied a chain of countries. Multinationals also occupy and operate from different countries. Is there a different between the two? This is yet to be seen and proved. And the Africans will be the best judges.

ARE MULTINATIONALS ACCEPTED OUTSIDE AFRICA?

Realizing the effects of multinationals in their country, the Americans have had different opinions, all portraying a strong opposition toward such powers. In a 1988 opinion survey carried by *The International Economy*, 74 percent of Americans felt that foreign investment has lessened U.S. economic independence.   Similarly 78 percent saw a need for a law restricting foreign ownership of businesses or investors to register with the Government (Thomas Omestan in Frieden and Lake 1991:209).

In Canada like in the United States, reaction towards foreign investments has been one of great concern. During the 1960s and 1970s, the Canadians were distressed over American penetration in its market. As a result, over 200,000 Canadians joined Independent

Canada Associations. By this time, however, foreign owner ship of Canada's manufacturing and energy industries was above 50 percent. This prompted the Canadian Government to create a screening agency to screen foreign acquisitions (p.209)

It is ironical how these countries would restrict foreign investments in their premises, yet the same countries are investing abroad in great concentration. A good example is the United States. In his book, 1967 best-selling book, *The American Challenge,* the French author, Jean-Jacques Servan-Schreiber warned that "fifteen years from now the world's third greatest industrial power, just after the United States and Russia, may not be Europe, but American industry in Europe" (in Frieden and Lake 1991:209). This predictions can be backed by the fact that the U.S. Government seems committed to foreign involvement to a larger extent. According to economist Robert Gilpin as pointed in *The Political Economy of International Relations* (1987), "Foreign direct investment has been considered a major instrument through which the United States could maintain its relative position in world markets, and the overseas expansion of multinational corporations has been regarded as a means to maintain America's dominant world economic position in other expanding economies" (p.210).

From the outcry of the Americans concerning the foreign investments, one would think the foreigners have taken a larger percentage of the economic assets. The outcry is said to be over stated than the reality. In his observation, Thomas Omestad, in his article *Selling off America* notes "today, foreigners own 4-5 percent of total U.S. assets. Foreign interests employ around 3 million Americans" or 3.5 percent of the American labor force. (p.211)

Major investors in the United States are Britain, Japan, Nether-lands, Canada, and West Germany respectively.

In recent years, the growth of foreign investments has intensified. This indicates the need for concern among the Americans. Foreigner have dominated some areas, but not others. For examples, 20 percent of total bank asset is foreign owned; 12 percent of manufacturing base; 25 - 30 percent of chemical industry assets; almost half of consumer electronics and cement industries while only less than 1 percent of agricultural land is foreign owned.

It is easy for multinational corporations to operate abroad without the mother country complaining. However, once the mother country feels threatened by corporations penetrating its market, then the common reaction is protectionism of the local market, a behavior well shown by United States and Japan. It demonstrates the pain of allowing or being controlled by foreigners. Analysts see the major concern of countries as the fear of reduced economic and political autonomy.

The pain of losing economic and political autonomy is well ex pressed by Senator Frank Murkowski (R-Alaska) as quoted by *New York Times,* December 30, 1985. He notes: "Once they own your assets, they own you". Of course nobody would like to be owned by another person, especially a foreigner whose future and prosperity you can't predict or rely on. Yet foreigners would dream and plan of controlling   the   economy,   political   and   social-technological development of host countries. Africa is in the process of sinking to the ideology of being sold off to multinationals whose interest are on the increase especially from Japan, Britain, France, Germany and United States.

CHAPTER EIGHT

MULTINATIONALS AND MARKET PLACE MAGIC IN THE 1980S

BY RICHARD S. NEWFARMER

This article, reflecting structuralist, or dependency, critiques of the international economy order, strongly questions the alleged benefits of multinational enterprise (MNEs) for developing countries. Newfarmer argues that the oligopolistic nature of MNEs may impose economic costs on host countries and that the goals of the MNEs may conflict with the developmental goals of the host. He therefore expects continued government attempts to control MNE activity.

On October 15, 1981, President Ronald Reagan unveiled his program for developing countries. It revolves around three themes closely related to multinational corporations: (1) Reliance on markets to stimulate growth and development; (2) reliance on the private sector to lead development; and (3) minimizing government "interference" in the market. The president put the matter succinty: "The societies which achieved the most spectacular, broad-based economic progress in the shorts period of time are (those that) ... believe in the magic of the marketplace".

Certainly a principal actor in the Reagan program is the multinational corporation. By reducing the official development assistance efforts, his program implicitly places a heavy burden on their corporate shoulders. But will unfettered markets and MNCs produce the most rapid and broadly shared development? In addressing this question, this paper first looks at international markets, including the flows of foreign direct investment to developing countries and then the more complex question of the distribution of gains from multinational investment. Second, it examines the effects of multinational investment on the pattern development. The discussion suggests that powerful economic and political forces usually trigger government intervention in MNC activities and the administration program will probably be received coolly in most developing countries. Since intervention usually results in bargaining between host government and MNCs, a final section speculates on MNC-host government relations. ...

INTERNATIONAL MARKETS AND GROWTH OF DEVELOPING COUNTRIES

President Reagan stated his position with eloquence in the Philadelphia speech: "Free people," he said, "build free markets that ignite dynamic development for everyone". But it is not always clear that market-led development always does benefit everyone-at least with the sense of equity and fairness implicit in orthodox trade theory. The issue of the distribution of gains from MNC -- related trade and investment between host country and home country as well as the internal distributional effect have been the subject of heated political and academic controversy during much of the 1960s and 1970s. Two lines of argument suggests that the international markets in which MNCs operate will not produce growth as rapidly as some more preferable mixture of host-government intervention and market functioning.

The first line of argument focuses on the workings of international capital and technology markets, and points out that the flows in these markets are highly uneven. That is, foreign direct and indirect investment goes to the richest of poor nations and not to the nations which need it most. ... Eighty seven percent of investment is concentrated in 14 to 132 developing countries-almost all of them oil exporters or wealthy semi-industrialized countries. This is a fair indication that technological transfers associated either with MNCs or sold independently are also quite concentrated.

The poorest 36 countries experienced economic growth rates of 1.6% during the 1960-1979 period, well below those of both the semi-industrialized countries (3.8%) and developed countries (4.0%). Moreover, World Bank projections show that the current account deficits of oil-importing countries will be between $70 and $85 billion over the next five years, of which $40 to $50 billion may be financed through private lending or direct investment. The shortfall must be financed largely through concessional aid. A policy which relies solely on private international capital and technology markets to produce growth in the poor countries will certainly accentuate the pain of their structural adjustment and not ameliorate poverty for much of the 1980s. ...

Even if markets' capital and technology were perfectly competitive, laissez faire policies would undoubtedly produce similar flows. This is because the distribution of world wealth generates patterns of effective demand that create the most profitable business opportunities in the wealthy countries. Greater wealth means larger markets, greater opportunities for specialization, and economies of scale in production. To the problem which income distribution poses for free-market failure: the positive externalities associated with higher levels of production and wealth. Income distribution and market failures indicate that free-market policies will probably not produce sufficiently rapid growth in the poorest countries to narrow the gaps in per capital income separating rich and poor countries in the coming decades.

A second line of argument is more complex and requires greater elaboration, for it lies at the root of many MNC -- host government conflicts as well as the ill-fated North-South dialogue during the 1970s. The argument is that international markets are systematically biased against developing countries in their distribution of gains from trade and investment. These biases are traceable in part to the very existence of nation-states, which put restrictions on the movement of products and factors, and to the failure of markets to be competitive. This is not to say that trade and investment do not produce economic gains for buying and selling countries. ... is the distribution of gains between developing and developed countries. ...

The contention is that imperfect international markets associated with MNC investment bias the distribution of gains against developing countries, ultimately requiring some government intervention for maximum growth.

Most economists in both the North and South give some credence to the fundamentally oligopolistic character of the MNCs. ... This view starts with the insight that the MNC brings not only capital or technology to developing countries, but a package of tangible and intangible assets. The package is unique to each firm and thus not readily imitated by would-be competitors, especially domestic firms whose superior knowledge of the local business environment would in other instances give them a competitive edge.

MNC control of this unique bundle therefore gives them a monopolistic advantage in all markets and, together with their ability to raise barriers to entry to further protect their advantage, creates a market with a limited number of sellers-oligopoly.

Oligopoly may in certain circumstances be associated with in creases in global welfare, such as when it leads to economies of scale, economies of internalization, or increases in innovation. On the other hand, individual countries are not concerned about global welfare, but national welfare, and desire to accumulate benefits locally. From the perspective of developing countries, oligopoly raises the possibility that the costs of obtaining the package of MNC-provided assets is higher than would occur under workably competitive conditions-or if the package were de-bundled and the assets bought separately.

Even viewed more narrowly from the vantage of the product cycle-thought of as "cycles of monopoly" rather than as markets ineluctably working toward greater competition ... successive waves of MNC market power may put developing countries at a distinct disadvantage in unregulated market transactions. This is because of developing countries more often sell their products of factors in competitive markets in their dealings with developed countries or MNCs, while MNCs presumably sell in oligopolistic markets.

IMPACTS ON MARKET STRUCTURE

There is in fact considerable evidence that MNCs operate in oligopolistic markets. For example, Fajnzylber and Martinez Tarrago found that in Mexico, MNCs sold 61% of their total sales in markets where the leading four plants accounted for 50% or greater of the market and less than 10% in markets where the four leaders held less than 25%; by comparison, Mexican firms sold only 29% in the highly concentrated markets and 33% in the low-concentration industries. More sophisticated econometric studies have found a strong correlation between concentration and various indicators of foreign participation. These facts, together with studies showing strong correlation between market structures internationally, suggests that foreign direct investment is the bridge that links concentrated market structures in various countries-except perhaps where the state intervenes to proscribe multinational investments as in Japan.

These indicators of oligopoly-four-firm concentration ratios and the like-miss another important deviation from workable competition, market power attributed to conglomerate organization. A conglomerate is a firm which operates in several product and geographic markets. Almost by definition then, MNCs are large multi-market firms and have at their disposal discretionary power unavailable to single-market firms. This includes the ability to cross-subsidize growth in one market with profits from another, to manipulate transfer prices on in-house product and factor flows between markets, to allocate production among alternative countries, and engage in international price discrimination. Differences in relative size of MNCs and their domestic competitors also create asymmetry in competition. This power may or may not be used in ways which correspond to the dictates of workable competitive markets. ...

Underlying this association between MNCs and oligopoly is a blend of behavioral and technological causes. Technologies of many modern MNC products play a dual role. Patented technology forms part of the unique package of assets that is the monopolistic advantage of MNCs in the market, and thus accords MNCs an absolute cost advantage over potential competitors. Also, production technologies generate economies of scale which create a scale barrier to entry and limit the number of producers a market can efficiently support. Economies stemming from the internalization of international flows of information may also act as a scale barrier. ...

But technology and economics of internalization are far from the sole source of MNCs' monopolistic advantage. Company behavior in advertising, acquisitions, and restrictive business practices are probably as important as technology in creating concentrated domestic market structures. Advertising (discussed further below) has been shown to have a positive association with concentration in econometric studies of Brazil, Malaysia, Mexico, the Philippines and other countries. UNCTAD's several studies on restrictive business practices serve to illustrate the importance of interlocking directorates, cross-subsidization, local cartels and foreclosure of supplies. Unlike patent or scale barriers associated with technology or information transfers, these sources of monopolistic advantage do not usually carry the social benefits that might otherwise offset their effects on market structure. In most cases, their net effect is to restrict competition and raise prices to consumers with little or no efficiency gains.

Another behavioral determinant of domestic market structure stems from the fact that domestic oligopolies dominated by subsidiaries are linked to a larger global network of rivalry. As a newly studied phenomenon, "international oligopoly" merits detailed consideration.

INTERNATIONAL OLIGOPOLY?

As foreign investment has grown, MNCs in the same industry find themselves in competition with ever more frequency with the same rivals in several national markets. ... That is, there may be only a few large companies in an industry so that one firm may look out across the international market and recognize its strategic interdependence with a firm based in another industrialized country, eventually facilitating collusive or parallel actions in markets around the world.

One can imagine several kinds of international oligopolistic behavior, including the formation of cartels, spheres of influence, and joint ventures to share markets, as well as oligopolistic reaction in investment strategies; one can also imagine local market effects stemming from international business practices. Let me recount briefly Shepherd's analysis of the history of the international cigarette industry to show how a few of these forms have direct consequences for market structure and performance in developing countries.

In the 1880s, mechanization provided the initial dynamism for consolidation and concentration in the United States. James Duke formed the powerful American Tobacco Company (ATC) and introduced "demand creation" marketing. He turned to foreign investment when it appeared in the 1890s that a wave of quasi-moralistic anti-cigarette publicity and the flood of machine-made cigarettes had led to stagnation in the US market. ATC tried to penetrate the British market where 10-15 small domestic firms competed. These firms, fearing the powerful ATC, banded together to form the Imperial Tobacco Co. (ITC). The resulting struggle among equals eventually ended in truce when in 1903 ATC and ITC decided to establish a world cartel to limit their competition and share markets in the world. They allocated to each other their home territories and established a joint venture to control markets in the third world, called British American Tobacco (BAT). This cartel lasted until US antitrust authorities required its dissolution in 1911. The divestiture arrangements severed management ties among the three companies, though it left some minority equity holdings in place.

But the story of international oligopoly in cigarettes hardly ended there. American producers continued to produce primarily for the US market, comprising perhaps one-half of the world demand. ITC continued to produce in England and some European markets, BAT continued to have free rein in the developing world. With minor deviations, these "spheres of influence" evolved and   lasted with surprising durability until the mid-1960s. Then, the Surgeon General's Report in 1964 and subsequent consumer awareness in the United States that cigarettes were linked to cancer and other diseases caused a dramatic fall in the growth for US producers. They could only react by diversifying within the United States and by investing in foreign markets. This precipitated a wave of foreign investment that impinged on traditional BAT territory. Thus, in sharp contrast to BAT, over 90% of the 150 overseas affiliates of US cigarette manufacturers were established after 1965. Yet the point is that for nearly seven decades some loose form of international oligopolistic behavior determined the number and source of producers in the major cigarette markets of the developing world. ...

MARKET STRUCTURE AND PROFITABILITY

A final link in the argument from imperfect international markets to uneven distribution of gains is profitability. Two questions about profitability are relevant: If our concern for the determinants of structure is sound, then structure should be a determinant of profitability. Second, MNCs should be related to higher profitability.

Although widely studied in the industrialized countries, the market structure-profits relationship is only now becoming a   concern for development economists. The 15 studies that exist for developing countries are of varied sophistication and use disparate data sets, but they have surprisingly consistent results: Nearly all show a fairly strong positive relationship between imperfect market structures-market concentration, product   differentiation, relative market share, and to a lesser extent barriers to entry-and profitability.

The evidence comparing the profitability of MNCs to local firms is mixed. The econometric studies find either no difference or the MNCs in fact report lower profits. Concentration and other market imperfections may thus be the prime factor determining profits, not "foreignness" per se. It is also possible that foreign firms are in fact more profitable but that transfer pricing reduces downward profits reported in the host country.

This evidence is by no means conclusive in proving the assertion that the international system is biased in favor of home countries in the distribution of the gains from MNC-related trade and investment in favor of developing countries. One always wishes for more reliable data, more widely accepted assumptions, and fewer exogenous influences. But the evidence is persuasive that (a) foreign investment is strongly and persistently linked to domestic oligopoly in the host country, and (b) that domestic oligopoly generates high profits for those fortunate enough to operate in these markets. The evidence is sufficiently strong, in my opinion, to throw the burden of proof on those in the administration and in academia who hold that this distribution of gains from MNC-related trade and investment is fundamentally "fair".

Ironically, domestic market structure is a variable that host governments are in a position to influence-through domestic antitrust policy, tariff policy and other industrial policies. This raises the critical question of the role of the state, addressed in detail below. The point to be made here, however, is that any policy of letting "free markets work" will probably produce uneven growth among countries and relegate to developing countries a smaller share of the gains from MNC-related trade and investment than would occur in the presence of government bargaining or de-packaging of MNC assets.

MNCS AND THE PATH OF DEVELOPMENT

The consequences of a policy that relies on MNCs as a prime mover of growth extend beyond the consideration of the international distribution of gains. One of the most important consequences to analyze is their dynamic effects on the nature of growth itself which products are produced, which technologies are employed, and how industries are to fit themselves into an increasingly inter dependent global system. MNCs, of course are not the sole actors in the growth process. But a policy which accords MNCs a central role must recognize their influence in forging the path of development.

The way economies grow, as distinct from the growth rate itself, has an impact on economic sovereignty and national income distribution. From the perspective of a host country, the path that will permit the greatest flexibility and control in dealing with the constraints imposed upon internal growth by the international economy is to be preferred, ceteris paribus, over alternatives, These constraints include the effects of cyclical fluctuations in demand for host country exports associated with growth or recession in the industrialized world, as well as the perennial foreign exchange shortages and technology deficiencies stemming from the process of late-exchange shortages and technology deficiencies stemming from the process of late-starting industrialization itself. The long-term distributional effects of the way an economy grows are also from a host-country perspective. The evolution of factor shares over time will depend on changes in relative factor quantities, changes in demand, the elasticity   of substitution between factors, and the factor bias in technical change. Government policy and institutional factors, such as the distribution of land or political power, are no less important in affecting income distribution of land or political power, are no less important in affecting income distribution. It is of more than passing interest to planners in host government how MNCs affect these relationships and with them the path of development.

One approach to the obviously difficulty measurement problems in addressing this issue is to study how MNCs "grow different" from domestic firms in an industry. Holding industry constant (and therefore government policy to the extent it is nondiscriminatory   among ownership groups), this comparison can often place differences in behavior in stark relief and we can see how the differences in firm behavior affect development. Let us consider five aspects of firm behavior: advertising, technological   appropriateness,   technological   dependence,   trade propensities, and transfer prices. All have implications for economic sovereignty and income distribution.

ADVERTISING

There are several reasons to suspect that MNCs may be associated with increasing levels of advertising. The promotion of certain products over others ultimately influences consumer choices and the mix of products available locally. First, an important monopolistic advantage of many MNCs is their differentiated products coupled with their superior marketing skills. These skills are usually employed to mount substantial advertising campaigns. Second, an element of differentiation in many consumer goods is constant change of model and product design, regard less of the actual usefulness of the change. Sometimes these costs are quite expensive, as in the auto industry. MNCs are the unquestioned leaders in this process as they ride the crest of the product-cycle wave, another element of their monopolistic advantage. Third, many of the new products are designed in the first instance for the mass markets of the home country, markets where wealth and consumer awareness are much higher, and where poverty is far less widespread, leading to questions about the appropriateness of products for poor countries.

Evidence on the issue of advertising is of three types. The first links MNCs to the parallel rise of the multinational advertising agencies. Both are seen as promoting the technology of inefficient consumption. These studies are not particularly helpful in isolating the role of MNCs from domestic actors, who after all use the same foreign advertising agencies. Second, some anecdotal and econometric evidence does seem to indicate that MNCs change promotional norms within an industry. For example MNCs sponsored 75-80% of radio and newspaper ads in Swahili and English in Kenya and were responsible for 45% of all advertising placed. Econometric findings for Brazil, Mexico, Malaysia, and the Philippines show that the level of foreign ownership was positively correlated with the level of industry advertising, though one study for a more limited sample in Colombia found no difference.

The third variety of evidence is case studies, and is perhaps the most persuasive because it charts the dynamic relation between increases in foreign ownership and changes in promotional norms and product quality. American firms entering Argentina's cigarette industry were responsible for a quadrupling of the advertising expenditures to sales in the three years after their entry in 1966. Other cases are also reported in Mexico's food industry and in pharmaceuticals for Argentina.

The much-discussed case of infant formula offers the clearest case of the link between the growth of multinationals, changes in promotional norms, and the link to inappropriate products. Nestle's activities in much of the Third World drew attention because the company used saleswomen dressed in white coats to promote sales of infant formula in rural areas. It became popular in several communities to switch from breast-feeding to formula, even at the increased cost of poor consumers. An ad verse side consequence in many areas, however, was an increase in infant mortality and malnutrition because mothers mixed the formula with polluted water; they were not able to sterilize their feeding implements; or they cut down the amount of milk powder in the formula mixture to save money. This illustrates the more general point that consumer ignorance is much higher in developing countries, consumer protection laws much weaker, and so the net distorting effects of MNC advertising in "consumption technology" may be greater.

While the evidence is not conclusive, the development implications of increases in advertising associated with foreign investment are extremely important. First, advertising appears to increase industrial concentration in developing countries, with attendant consequences for income distribution and economic efficiency. Second, advertising appears to influence profitability, as discussed above, channeling more resources for investment in the differentiated consumer goods-industries that tend to produce goods serving the relatively wealthy. Third, advertising does appear to direct consumer choice towards the advertised products and therefore shift consumption patterns to mirror those in the North, shaping the "ideology of consumption". Advertising levels in developing countries are now comparable to those in the developed countries. ...

Product choice has a strong impact on the path of development because it influences which industries are established and, to the extent that elasticities of substitution between labor and capital are less than one, which technologies are employed. This had direct implications for distribution and economic sovereignty.

TECHNOLOGICAL APPROPRIATENESS

Because MNCs create technology in an environment where capital is cheap relative to labor, it has been argued that their technology is probably more capital-intensive than is appropriate to developing countries. The transfer of their technology on the heels of their products, the argument runs, creates a bias in growth towards a capital-intensive technology with its adverse effects on employment and income distribution. Despite the large number of studies on the relative labor intensity of multinationals and domestic firms, there are to date a few definitive results. ...

One reason why this question is so difficult to resolve is that technological change is bound up closely with changes in products. Cutting in at any point in time for measurement probably misses imitation effects among ownership groups when a new product or technology is introduced, diluting any statistical results. Also, controlling for product mix and quality is extremely difficult in cross-sectional studies. The most promising area of further research is that of case studies linking the introduction of new products and advertising with changes in technology and market structure.

In conclusion, it should be noted that variation in capital-labor ratios is far more sensitive to industry that to ownership group, suggesting the policy instrument of greatest importance is   the selection of which industries are to be established, and only secondarily who produces within any given industry.

Source: Copyright (c) 11/90
>   From: *International Political Economy*, 2
>   By: Freiden/Lake
>   Reprinted with permission of St. Martin's Press, Inc.

CHAPTER NINE

TECHNOLOGICAL DEPENDENCE
BY NEW FARMER

Technological dependence refers to the continuing inability of a developing country to generate the knowledge, inventions, and innovations necessary to propel self-sustaining growth. If a country does not produce its own technology in at least some industries, it is argued, it will suffer slower growth and more disadvantageous terms of trade in the long run. As the product-cycle model suggests, technological prowess is often the secret to large shares in fast-growing export markets and to some degree of market power, and hence high prices. Developing countries have long recognized that the inability to produce a local technology can hamper economic growth. ... Technological dependence may mean slower or "distorted" growth and reduced economic sovereignty.

Magee, for one, sees MNCs as behaving differently in their approach to local knowledge creation. MNCs create "information" with the hope of appropriating some portion of the prospective monopoly rent associated with the application of the patented information in production and marketing. Since patent protection is imperfect, MNCs are predicted to develop technology for markets where barriers to entry may be expected to supplement patent protection. It follows from Magee's argument that MNCs will transfer technology to developing countries within those institutional frameworks that maximize "appropriable" rents (most desirable the wholly owned subsidiary) and when business conditions make such a transfer the most profitable (usually in response to tariffs, government demands, or threats to the local markets formerly served by exports). It also follows that MNCs will generally prefer to tightly control research and development activities, the source of new information, in the home country. Centralization of the R & D activities of the global company conflicts directly with the interests of developing countries in domestic technological "party" and independence. ...

Perhaps the most persuasive case of seeing MNCs as the institutionalization of technological dependence comes from the experience of Japan, which did not permit the establishment of MNC subsidiaries. After World War II, the Japanese continued their policy of not permitting foreign direct investment but of spending liberally for imported licensed technology. Their purchase of technology from abroad were considerable, yet at the same time they spent more than four times that amount on domestic R & D. Within the relatively short period of two decades they trans formed themselves into aggressive world leaders in many industries. It is arguable that this would not have occurred had US and European MNCs been allowed to control technology-intensive industries in Japanese manufacturing.

TRADE

MNCs' international trade behavior appears to be different as well. With import substitution industrialization, MNCs may initiate local production through the assembly of imported components and then gradually shift to local inputs as supplier industries develop and relative costs shift in favor of local purchase. However, MNCs may lag domestic firms in the process of domestic integration for several reasons: Local inputs may entail risks in quality and supply; parents profit on the export of parts to captive subsidiaries; costs may be different due to economies of scale; exports to subsidiaries from the parent facilitate the accumulation of profits abroad through transfer pricing; and exports from the home country please home governments worried about trade deficits and employment. Domestic firms have different interests in nearly all of these areas. On the other hand, if wide cost differences between local and foreign inputs persist, local producers may join foreign producers in opposing domestic vertical integration.

These dynamics do appear to lead to higher import propensities for foreign subsidiaries than for domestic firms, even among firms in the same industry. Although some studies have shown no difference, the majority point to higher import propensities.

One might expect that an elevated import propensity for MNCs would in some measure be offset by higher export propensities.   MNCs have marketing channels in place, know foreign markets   better than domestic competitors, and may be better able to take   advantage of inter-country difference in costs of production. On the other hand, it could be that with production facilities   already in place in several markets, parents would discourage   subsidiary exports on the ground that such exports would be competitive with existing operations.

A review of the several studies of relative export performance   supports only weak generalizations.   Several show that domestic   firms perform somewhat better.   An exception is when the government has taken carrot-and-stick measures to create incentives for   MNCs to export. ... Another important variable influencing MNC   exports from developing countries is the degree of competition   experienced in the home country. The aggressive Japanese en trance to the US electronics industry, for example, led American   firms to respond by setting up "export platforms" in several   developing countries to take advantage of lower labor costs. These situations illustrate the importance of MNC links to the   home market in determining firm behavior in the developing country.

TRANSFER PRICING

Since the sale of a good or a service from one affiliate to   another is not subject to the discipline of the market, the   appropriate authority in the corporate hierarchy is free to set   prices at the most advantageous level for maximizing corporate   profits subject to effective constraints imposed by governments.   Intra-firm trade of MNCs accounts for a significant share of manufactured imports and exports of most developing countries.   There are several reasons why MNCs might find it advantageous to manipulate transfer prices by over pricing imports to host countries or underpricing exports: to avoid controls on profit repatriation, on royalties payments and on local prices (because inflated import prices show up as higher costs), or to circumvent   local tax rules, tariffs, exchange rate controls.   The incentives   are usually present to use transfer prices against developing countries because taxes in developing countries are often higher,   import duties on intermediate goods lower, currencies are less stable, and controls on profit remittances more stringent. The recent precipitous cuts in US corporate taxes under the Reagan administration have probably widened the tax rate differences.

Since Vaitsos' seminal study that found that overpricing of intra-firm exports to affiliates amounted to more than 15% of the world prices in four Colombia industries, a few other studies have indicated that MNCs do indeed take advantage of the mechanism. Robins and Stobaugh developed an optimization model of MNCs operating under different tax regimes and found that manipulating transfer prices could increase global profits as much as 15%. Their interviews of several companies found that managers of large MNCs were not taking full advantage of transfer prices, though medium-size companies tended to be more aggressive in seeking out transfer pricing profits. More recently the Greek government, for example, found that foreign subsidiaries on average paid 20% higher than the world market price in their sample of metallurgical imports and 25.7% for chemical imports. ...

This cursory review of five important dimensions of MNC behavior suggests that there is a strong reason to believe that MNCs alter the character of growth in ways that do not always promote broadly shared development. It is entirely possible that their effects on changing the aggregate pattern of demand through advertising, combined with their effect in biasing the factor-intensity of technologies and in shaping market structures that accompany the new products, aggravate income inequities. These tendencies probably more than offset any tendencies stocks and hence lower returns to capital relative to labor. Similarly, there is reason to believe that the trade effects do not contribute to greater economic sovereignty or to structures of trade like to produce the greatest gains in development.

All this is not easy to say that MNCs do not have a contribution to make to development. To the contrary, often they represent the most immediately available combination of valuable resources. Rather, the conclusion to be drawn from this discussion is that there is much legitimate and well-founded concern about the influence of MNCs on market-led development, and, from the host government's perspective, much to be gained from bargaining vigorously with MNCs.

For that reason, host governments will in all likelihood continue to pressure MNCs for a greater share of the gains from their activities and for changes in their behavior. A US policy that asks host governments to reduce their regulatory role vis-a-vis MNCs thus flies in the face of some powerful political-economic forces.

MNCS AND THE STATE: A NEW ERA OF PEACEFUL COEXISTENCE?

A strong argument can be made for the idea that the era of Nationalism and MNC-host government conflict is passed. Some authors have suggested that bargaining power in the bilateral negotiations between states and MNCs has swung irreversibly in favor of host governments, producing a new, more equitable distribution of gains and with it a new stability. Indeed, several studies of the natural resource industries show that after the huge fixed costs of investments in resource installations are sunk, the host government can in effect "hold the company hostage". Bargains made at entry become obsolete as power shifts from the companies to the state.

At the same time, the technical expertise within the governments to negotiate beneficial contracts has strengthened the governments' bargaining hand. Governments have learned to play off one oligopolist against another. Governments in the Caribbean succeeded in getting Kaiser to break the united opposition of the larger aluminum companies to govern participation in their bauxite operations. The Brazilians were able to set up an air craft industry by creating a state enterprise and buying licenses from Piper, the weaker competitor of Cessna. Cessna had dominated the Brazilian market but it refused government demands to take on domestic partners and begin local production with international technology.

Also, the explosion of international liquidity as petrodollars were recycled through the Eurodollar markets has given host governments an alternative to MNC-provided capital. Between 1970 and 1980, foreign direct investment fell from 34% of nonconcessional flows going to developing countries to 27%, while private bank and bond lending rose from 30% to 36%. In the short period between 1978 and 1980, the claims of American banks on Third World nations rose from $78 billion to $137 billion. It is argued that this has strengthened the hand of host governments in dealing with MNCs.

MNCs, for their part, have demonstrated a new flexibility in their dealings with host governments. This has given rise to unprecedented arrangements in technology transfer and ownership arrangements. One indication of this is the trend toward joint ventures. It is probable that the increase in joint ventures is largely attributable to post-1973 increases in Japanese foreign investment in natural resources in partnership with governments. Joint ventures in manufacturing, undoubtedly more common than a decade ago, are still by and large majority-controlled, with stock dispersed on incipient local capital markets or in the hands of weak joint-venture partners.

Nonetheless, the importance of joint ventures should not be overlooked because in the industrialized countries these have historically provided a stepping-stone to full domestic control later. The same could be said for other 'new forms' of multinational activity, such as management contracts and engineering and services.

Yet it would be a mistake to infer from these changes a new era of peaceful coexistence in MNC-host country relations. The thrust of the analysis in the first part of this paper suggests that governments will continue to apply pressure to MNCs to increase their share of the gains from multinational investment, to overcome foreign exchange and technology constraints, and, perhaps with less urgency, to spread the benefits of development. Measures taken range from regulating firm conduct, such as in the transfer of patented technology and requiring exports as a condition for importing, to squeezing MNCs out of industries by systematically favoring domestic or state enterprises over foreign subsidiaries.

To be sure, the parameters of bargaining are considerably narrower than in the 1960s from the viewpoint of both host countries and MNCs. Host countries are more appreciative of the full costs of nationalization and less disposed to rapid expropriation. Companies, for their part, realize that a piece of the market is better than none at all; it may even be embarrassing when a hard- line stance by one oligopolist is broken with a concession of a competitor, who then enjoys the more limited fruits of the bar gain; and collusive stances vis-à-vis an aggressive government are arguably more difficult to forge in an international (as opposed to an American) oligopoly. The massive expansion of private international debt has undoubtedly reinforced this parameter on the company side. The international banks, many of which have intimate ties with industrial companies, have a vested interest in the overall macroeconomics success of the developing country. They cannot simply shut down a plant and pull out in a dispute over a single investment or policy; rather they must rely on negotiated outcomes or risk losing an entire portfolio. But the underlying drive within the narrower bargaining parameters continues to be for developing countries to change the structure of their economies, compelling most host countries to pressure the MNCs.

In this view, the primary reason that MNC-host conflicts have abated in the late 1970s is the weakened (not strengthened) position of many states brought about by the abrupt price in creases in oil. Developing countries which coped with the oil-induced problems of structural adjustment by borrowing recycled   petrodollars were soon dealt a second blow-abrupt increases in world interest rates. These two events have turned terms of trade sharply against oil-importing developing countries, and   their current-account deficits moved deeply into the red. Thus, even though commercial bank lending increased in relative share of capital inflows into these countries, foreign investment inflows are no less important for their contribution to capital- account balances. (In fact, with the abrupt rise and instability   in international interest rates, governments may well prefer equity over debt as a source of capital). Any government action   to undermine the position of foreign investors during this period jeopardizes this thin stream of inflows.

These events weakened major nationalists initiatives to change ownership and other relationships with MNCs in Latin America and elsewhere. Brazil, the largest single recipient of foreign inflows among developing countries and one of the most sophisticated regulators of multinational investment, slowed its attempts to leverage industries out of MNC control. The Andean Pact abandoned its Article 24 agreement requiring a fade-out of foreign investment for a mixture of reasons: Chile's withdrawal from the pact after the military coup in 1973, the impact of the foreign exchange shortage induced by the deterioration in terms of trade, and finally the political difficulty of implementing the accords in multiple countries. The change in governments in Peru after 1975 in the face of severe economic recession, together with the change in Chilean policy and the subsequent defeat of Manley in Jamaica, gave rise to the feeling that, among their other "mistakes", the nationalistic regimes in these countries had pressed their bargaining position vis-à-vis the companies too   far. Their experience argued for subtlety in negotiation.

Besides the weakening of states attributable to the international economy, the very spread of MNCs in manufacturing has also had an impact upon the internal politics of the state in a way that   places new constraints on the "political will" to bargain, and thus requires technocrats use greater finesse in future bargaining.   Contrary to the case in raw-materials production, MNCs in   manufacturing have far greater linkages to local interest groups-MNCs employ a larger labor force (per unit of capital) than most   raw-materials ventures, they usually create a larger network of white-collar employees, and they usually have at least a few domestic competitors who share broad class interests (though not without conflict at the margin). These social groups have much deeper roots in civil society than do elites traditionally associated with raw materials. This makes "foreigners"
much less obvious targets of nationalistic forces on the one hand, and on the other, accords them some influence in policy makers' circles...

Also contrary to the raw materials case, a continual flow of new products and technology emanates from the home country so that the subsidiaries' continued growth and prosperity is contingent to some degree upon its links to the parent. This works to strengthen the hand of multinational manufacturers of differentiated products over time....

A final change in business organization in the 1970s also places a new parameter on the political will of the state: Many advanced developing countries have sired their own multinationals, giving their governments a new stake in an open international commercial system. This tendency is rapidly growing but small in relative importance and so is not yet strong enough to dampen the overall impulse of host governments to bargain.

These two socioeconomic dynamics-a drive for host governments to change the structure of their economies in the face of market pressures to the contrary and narrowing bargaining parameters- will undoubtedly play themselves out differently in each country. Given the narrow parameters of bargaining in manufacturing, government strategies will probably be more stable, more piece meal, and slower than the over conflicts of the past that some times ended in nationalization of the toppling of a regime-or both. ...

One element... may figure prominently in MNCs-host country relations and is wholly unpredictable: the politics supporting the regimes in advanced developing countries. The current path of developing continues to leave large numbers of people isolated from the benefits of development. Unemployment, malnutrition, and low productivity continue to characterize large segments of the population, even in advanced developing countries. To be sure, these groups are not wholly unaffected by growth; the better among them are not infrequently able to climb above some line of absolute poverty during their lifetimes. Nonetheless, concepts of social justice and human rights to the basic necessities of life often precede the economic model's capacity to deliver them, sowing the seeds of political change. This is especially true of urban poor, who are most susceptible to the new aspirations for consumption introduced by advertising and most vulnerable to downturns in growth rates. These politics may interact with slow real growth in many developing countries... to produce a volatile mixture of political instability. In some countries, these politics will certainly reshape the parameters of negotiation between the state and multinational companies in the coming years.

Source: Copyright (c) 11/90
    From: *International Political Economy*, 2
    By: Freiden/Lake
    Reprinted with permission of St. Martin's Press, Inc.

CHAPTER TEN

AFRICANS BLAST EUROPEAN BEEF DUMPING: SAHEL LIVESTOCK TRADE IN RUINS

BY KAREN GELLEN

As West African countries lodge increasingly sharp protests against the European Community's policy of dumping cheap beef on the regional market, the EC is responding with token concessions. Heavily subsidized exports of frozen beef from European are flooding markets in countries such as Burkina Faso, Niger and Mali, provoking a breakdown of the indigenous regional livestock trade.

At mid-year the EC agreed to cut 15 per cent from the handsome $2.40 a kilo subsidy and analyze the effect by year's end. Critics of the subsidy, which has amount to $420 million over the past nine years, argue that the move will have scant effect on the export tide. They say the 50,000 tones the EC estimates will go to West Africa annually under the new terms is an insignificant reduction from the 54,000 tones sold in 1991. They urge a 50 per cent cutback for starters, and an ultimate phase- out of the subsidy.

The gristly cuts of poor quality beef, which have few takers in Europe, are undercutting West African market prices by as much as 50 per cent, threatening the livelihood of some 4 million local livestock herders. Urban-dwellers in the region -- who readily purchase the cheap meat - are endangered in turn by difficulties in safely handling frozen food and by the exports' poor nutritional content.

For pastrolists in Burkina Faso, the dumping has proved devastating. "Everything here relies on the income from selling animals," says agricultural official Jean-Marie Kabore. In the dry, often barren Sahel, he notes, "no one can count on crop production". Kabore's comment appears in Brussels Beef Carve-Up, a 1993 study by the London-based charity Christian Aid, which terms the EC's subsidy rules a "scandal."

Peter Madden, author of the report, told African Farmer that the European agricultural policies have an "entirely negative" impact on developing countries. He cites limited access for exports from Africa, downward pressure on world market prices and an undermining of African farmers' incomes. Madden adds that dumping promotes a "taste for inappropriate foreign food" that is initially cheap but, after edging out local commodities, can become an expensive item.

West African governments have fought back by imposing tariffs on the beef imports, but the region's permeable borders enable European sellers to circumvent the regulations. Cote d'Ivoire's import levy coincided, for example, with a fourfold jump in imports to neighboring Ghana. "We're sure the meat wasn't staying in Ghana - it was going straight across the border," says Madden,   who adds that the dumping exacerbates regional differences. EC policy "plays off" poor Sahelian producer countries against wealthier coastal nations, he maintains, with urban residents getting cheap prices at the expense of small-scale farmers.

EC countries also have competing interest. Last year alone, Europeans paid $354 billion in farm subsidies through taxes and price hikes. In the current fight over reform of the EC's Common Agricultural Policy, England, with only 2 percent of its workforce in farming, has little political stake in subsidies, unlike France, where 15 percent work the land.

Christian Aid notes, meanwhile, that few European farmers would suffer from elimination of the beef subsidy, as exports to West Africa represent less than 0.5 per cent of total EC production. The policy meanwhile undermines EC-sponsored livestock development projects, including building modern slaughterhouses in Burkina Faso and helping breed improved herds in Mali, Cote d'Ivoire and Ghana.

The report is part of a drive by Christian Aid and other European non-governmental organizations to change EC policy. At the same time, the report notes, West African governments must cooperate to protect the regional market.

Although Burkina Faso's Kabore is pessimistic about early action in that direction, he maintains that West Africans could indeed forge a mutually beneficial policy, while alerting public opinion to what beef dumping is doing to the region.

AN END TO AFRICA'S EXPORT PRICE SLIDE?

BY ROY LAISHLEY

African farmers will be hoping that the World Bank has got it right. In its latest commodity projections, the Bank forecasts a break in the 20-year downward slump in export prices, which have taken many to their lowest levels ever. According to its Global Economic Prospects, issued in April, a combination of improving world economic growth and the shift of some developing countries towards more exports of processed goods should prompt a stabilization in real terms of raw material prices from next year onwards.

A detailed examination of the Bank's projections, however, makes it clear that any gain for producers will be small. And the Bank warns that prices will remain volatile, with a high risk of further decline if the anticipated growth in the world economy fails to materialize. Even on current forecasts, the Bank's real price index for agricultural products will still be below 1990 levels at the end of the century.

Price performance so far this year has been mixed. While sisal, sugar and tea have all risen in nominal terms compared with the first half of last year, most agricultural product prices have been stagnant or sharply down.

Cocoa prices are down 9 per cent this year, but the decision by Cote d'Ivoire to withhold part of this season's crop helped raise prices in July. News that Latin American coffee producers are to withhold supplies from the market has given some buoyancy to an otherwise weak market. African coffee producers are working to get a new international agreement on prices, but face an uphill task. With Asian producers set to overtake them as the largest suppliers of robusta coffee, African exporters' influence on the world market is weakening.

Falling Asian sugar production - and a smaller Cuban crop - helped prices of that commodity rise 12 per cent in the first half of the year. But with many African countries still heavy importers, this is a mixed blessing.

The World Bank is predicting a sharp rise for both groundnut and palm oil in 1994 in real terms, with coffee prices also expected to improve. These, however, are the only clear winners. More modest increases are forecast for cocoa, cotton, maize, rice and sugar, while citrus, tea and tobacco are projected to fall further.

Sources of the two articles: Karen Gellen. *African Farmer.* New York, October 1993. PP. 44-5. Used by permission of The Hunger Project; Roy Laishley - Managing Director. *Africa Recovery,* a United Nations quarterly Magazine, (in *African Farmer* October, 1993, P. 45.

BIBLIOGRAPHY AND OTHER REFERENCES

Acknowledgment: Sections Reprinted with permission of Simon and Schuster from *The Lonely African* by Colin M Turnbull. Copyright 1962 by Colin M. Turnbull, copyright renewed 1990 by Colin M. Turnbull

Adams. William Y. *Nubia -- Corridor to Africa.* London, 1977.

African Farmer October, 1993, P. 45.

Africa Today. "The OAU at 25: The Quest For Unity, Self-Determination and Human Rights". Vol. 35, Nos 3 & 4, 1983, 3rd & 4th Quarters, January 15th, 1989.

African Report. "Drought Destroying The Seeds of Democracy". New York; May - June, 1992.

Akintoye, S. A. *Emergent African States: Topics in Twentieth Century African History.* London: Longman Group, 1976.

Bennerman, Helen. *The Story of Little Black Sambo.* Britain, 1898.

Bennet, Gordon James. *New York Herald.* 19__

Berrill, Kenneth (ed). *Economic Development With Special Reference to East Asia.* London: 1964.

Bovill, E. W. *The Golden Trade of The Moors.* New York, 1958

Brett, E. *Colonialism and Underdevelopment in East Africa.* New York: NOK Publisher, 1973.

Brooke, James. *New York Times.* September 13, 1987.

Brown, Lester R., Alan Durning, Christopher Flavin, Lori Heise,   Jedi
          Jacodson, Sandra Prostel, Michael Renner, Cnythia Pollock
          Shea and Linda Starke. *State of the World: A Worldwatch Institute
          Report on Progress Toward a Sustainable Society.* New York: W.
          W. Norton and   Company, 1989.

Curtain, Philip, Steve Fierman Leonard Thompson and Jan Vansine.
          African History. London: Longman Group (U.K.) Ltd, 1988.

Davidson, Basil. "The Cockpit of the World*". African Guide: World of
          Information.* England: World of Information, 1979.

Endel - Jakob Kolde. *Environment of International Business.* Boston,
          Massachusetts: Kent Publishing Company, 1985.

Fage, J.D. (Ed). *The Cambridge History of Africa: C. 500 B.C. To
          A.D. 1050, Vol.2.* Cambridge, 1978.

Forrester, Marion. *The Economic and Social Relationship Between
          The Urban African Worker and The Rural Areas:
          Preparatory Paper for the Thessolonica Conference.*
          Nairobi: East Africa Statistical Department, 1959.

Frieden, Jeffry A. and David A. Lake. *International Political
          Economy.* New York: St. Marin Press, 1991.

Galbraith, John Kenneth. *The Vocie of The Poor: Essays In Economic and
          Political Persuasion.* Havard University, Press, 1983.

Gallen, Karen. Africans Blast European Beef Dumping. *African
          Farmers.* New York, October, 1993.

Gordon, Rene. *Africa: A Continent Revealed.* Nairobi: Camerapix, 1988.

Green, Reginald H. and Ann Seldman. *Unity or Poverty? The
          Economic of Pan-Africanism.* Harmondesworth: Penguin
          Book, 1968.

Gregory, Knight C. and James L. Newman. *Contemporary Africa
          Geography and Change.* New Jersey: Englewood Cliffs;
          Prentice-Hall, Inc. 1976.

Grove, A. T. *Africa.* London: Oxford University Press, 1979.

Habbard, James. *Atlantic Monthly,* March, 1910.

Hall, Martin. *Settlement Patterns In The Iron Age of Zululand: An Ecological Interpretation.* Oxford, 1980.

Hallet, Robin. *Africa Since 1975: A Modern History.* Nairobi: Heinemann, 1980.

Hancock, Graham (ed.). *Africa Guid: World of Information*, 1980. England: World of Information, 1980.

Harbison, Fredrick and Charles A. Meyers. *Educating Manpower and Economic Growth.* New York: McGraw-Hill, 1964.

Harris, Nigel. *The End of the Third World: Newly Industrializing Countries and The Decline of An Ideology.* New York: Penguis Books, 1987.

Harrison, Paul. *The Greening of Africa: Breaking Through In the Battle For Land and Food: An International Institute For Environment And Development - Earthiscan Study.* Washington D.C. Penguin Books, 1987. CMT, New York: 1962.

Khambata, Dara. *International Business Theory and Practice.* New York: Macmillan Publishing company, 1992.

Kevin Shilington. *History of Africa.* London: Macmillan Publishers, 1989.

Kindleberger, Charles P. and Bruce Herrick. *Economic Development.* New York. McGraw Hill Books Company, 1977.

Laishley, Roy. `And End to Africa's Export Price Slide?' *African Farmer,* New York, October 1993.

Marrison, Donald George, Robert Cameron Mitchell, John Naber Paden and Hugh Michael Stevenson. *Black Africa: A Comparative Handbook.* New York: The Free Press Ltd, 1972.

Mazrui, Ali. A. and Michael Tidy. *Nationalism and States In Africa: From about 1937 to the Present.* Nairobi: Heinemann Kenya, 1989.

Mbugua, Bedan. `Principles Leadership', *The Option.* Nairobi, February, 1995.

Muoria, Henry. *The Gikuyu And The White Fury.* Nairobi: East African Educational Publisher, 1994.

Murkowski, Frank (Senator-Alaska) *New York times,* December 30, 1985.

Nkrumah, Kwame. *Neo-Colonialism, The Last Stage of Imperialism.* London: Heinemann, 1968.

Odhiambo Thomas R., Anyang' Nyong'o, Emmanuel Hansen, Godfrey Lardrer and Dustain Wai. *Hope Born Out of Despair: Managing The African Crisis.* Nairobi: Heinemann, 1988.

Oliver Roland and A. Almore. *Africa Since 1800.* Cambridge University Press, 1967.

Oliver, Roland, (ed). *The Cambridge Encyclopedia for Africa.* London: Cambridge University Press, 1981.

Oliver, Roland. *The Dawns of African History.* New York: 1986.

Oliver, Roland and Brian Fagan. *Africa In The Iron Age: C. 500 B.C. to A.D. 1400.* Cambridge, 1975.

Oliver, Roland and Michael Crowder (editors). *The Cambridge Encyclopedia of Africa.* New York: Cambridge University Press, 1981.

Paden, John N. and Edward W. Soja (ed.). *The African Experience Volume I Essays.* Evanston: Northwest University Press, 1970.

Phillepson, D.W. *The Early Pre-History of Eastern and Southern Africa.* London, 1977.

Pollard, Sidney. *Wealth and Poverty: An Economic History of The Twentieth Century.* New York: Oxford University Press, 1990.

Posnansky, Merricks. *Prelude to East African History* London: 1977.

P. T. Ellsworth, *The International Economy.* New York: Macmillan, 1964.

Shaw, Thurstan C. *Nigeria: Its Archaelogy and Early History.* England:Longman House, 1988.

Shillington, Kevin. *History of Africa.* London: Macmillan Pub. Ltd., 1989.

Stain, Jacquiline. *The Constitution of Ancient Greece.* NewYork: Holt, Rinehart and Winston, Inc. 1971.

The World Book Encyclopedia (A) Vol 1. Chicago: World Book - Childcraft International, Inc. 1980.

Tumbull, Colin M. *The Lonely African*. New York: Simon and Schuster, 1962.

Unger, Sanford J. *Africa: The People of an Emerging Continent*.
New York: Simon and Schuster, Inc. 1989.

Walter, T. W. Alastair M. Taylor and Nels M. Bailkey. *Civilization Past & Present Volume one (7 ed.)*. Glenview, Illinois. Scott, Foresman and Company, 1976.

Wolstenholme, G.E.W. *Man and Africa,* 1965.

Worcester, J.H. Jr. *David Livingston: First To Cross Africa With The Gospel*. Chicago: Moody Press, 19__

World Bank Statistical Yearbook, 1978. Washington D.C., 1978

World Bank, World Development Report, 1984. New York: Oxford University Press, 1984.

World Development Report 1990. Poverty: World Development Indicators. The World Bank. Washington D.C. Oxford University Press, 1990.

World Development Report 1991: The Challenge of Development: World Development Indicator. Washington D. C. Oxford University Press, 1991.

INDEX

Author Bibliography

Samuel Muriithi is a Lecturer in the Department of Commerce, Daystar University, Nairobi, Kenya. Born in Kenya, Sam received his education both Kenya and the United States of America. He has a Master of Business Administration degree (MBA) from the School of Business and Economics, Seattle Pacific University, a Master of Arts in Communications (MA), from Wheaton Graduate School, and a Bachelor of Arts degree in Business Administration and Management from Messiah College. His area of concentration include African Economic Problems, Management, Economics, International Trade and development. Sam has served as a research consultant in Africa in areas of management and communication. He is also the author of several articles and books. Seeing much need to promote African as a continent, Sam now focuses his attention to African development dilemma.